To Dad.

A growing boy couldn't ask
for a better role model.
And a fortysomething man couldn't ask
for fonder memories.

CONTENTS

You Are an Exception!
If you're a man, and if you are reading this, you're an exception to a rule.

You see, the book industry often quotes studies showing that 70 to 80 percent of today's book buyers are women. In other words, we men do not read books.

So when Tyndale House Publishers and I published *The Total Man* back in the late 1970s, we took quite a chance.

And struck a nerve. Men did buy that book. On top of that, wives bought it for husbands. Girlfriends bought it for boyfriends, and mothers bought it for sons. All to the tune of nearly 200,000 copies—which I'm told is something of a milestone for a book written to men, who do not read books.

Then the mail came. Men wrote me to say thanks for sharing some things they needed to hear. Women wrote to say thanks for helping their men understand and love them better. Couples wrote to say they had fallen more deeply in love since reading the book.

Feedback like that always makes the

effort seem worthwhile. And it's true that we men need to continue encouraging each other. We live in a world where values are easily skewed and ethics are too situational. We're concerned about doing our best at work and providing for our loved ones. Rising costs, increased demands on our time and energy, job pressures, church or community commitments—if we're not careful, all these can preoccupy us to the point where we're just slogging through instead of enjoying life to the fullest.

And if we're not careful, it's very possible that the most important human relationship in our world might get shoved to the bottom of the priority list: our relationship with that precious, priceless, one-of-a-kind masterpiece God created with a smile on his face.

A woman.

A very special woman.

So, in view of the challenges we men continue to face, Tyndale House and I are taking another chance with a book for men, who still supposedly do not read books.

Honest conversations, man to man, on three very important areas of a man's life: his mission, his money, his mate.

ManTalk.

We're confident that these pages contain dozens of practical, real-life ideas that can help you enjoy your work more, succeed with your money, and fall in love all over again with that special woman God has given you.

And to help you put it to work, we've provided practical suggestions for "Taking Action" at the end of each chapter. I know several men who are working through them right now. Others have told me they are forming breakfast discussion groups to motivate and encourage each other in these three areas of male life.

Enjoy the journey.

And thank you for being an exception. In all of life, may we all be.

PART ONE

Making the Most of Your Work

It's not a successful climb unless you enjoy the journey.

ON REACHING MOUNTAINTOPS

In the time of your life, live.
WILLIAM SAROYAN

Do you enjoy the thrill of accomplishment? I surely do.

My wife, Kathy, will tell you that one of the delights of my life is being able to cross a job off my list as "complete." Sometimes I become so focused on an objective that it's as if I'm wearing a set of invisible blinders so nothing can distract me.

I tend to carry this single-mindedness into recreational pursuits as well. One of my passions is to gather a few buddies, strap on a backpack, and set out for the summit of a 14,000-foot mountain. Reaching the mountaintop is an indescribable feeling of footsore, bone-weary, heart-pounding euphoria. If time allows, we'll camp at the top, sleeping under the stars, higher than anyone else in the country.

While climbing mountains, I

used to be so focused on reaching the summit that I would fix my eyes on the dirt path just a few feet in front of me, place one boot in front of the other, and suffer all kinds of agony in order to "make good time" up the mountain. Stop and rest? We'll rest when we get there! Admire the view? Just wait till we get to the top!

I lived for the accomplishment . . . the summit arrival. The trip up was just a long, dusty hassle I had to endure to reach the mountaintop.

I enjoyed the destination, but didn't allow myself to enjoy the journey.

THE LESSON OF LONG'S PEAK

On one of these mountain hikes, I learned an important lesson about achievements and success.

One bright Colorado-October day, a couple of friends and I set out for the top of Long's Peak. But after we had hiked an hour or so, our pristine blue sky was suddenly elbowed aside by a horde of angry, black storm clouds. Within moments we were engulfed by thick fog and icy snow. Our eyes stung as high winds whipped the snow into our faces. Before long we were walking in several inches of snow . . . and the storm was just beginning.

For a while we actually enjoyed the macho adventure of climbing onward and upward through the hostile elements. But when the storm showed no sign of letting up, we admitted we had to turn back. Stronger climbers had lost their lives on this mountain, in storms just like this one. So, reluctantly, we turned around and trudged down the mountain. We had set out for the peak and were denied.

For a few moments I was disgusted that the weather had kept us from our goal. I thought the trip was a failure—I would not be able to cross Long's Peak off my list this day.

But as we descended to our campsite, something dawned on me. Although we had missed the summit, this was quite an adventure! My friends and I were having a great time. It was an opportunity to blow urban soot out of our lungs, drink in the sights and smells of God's creation, get some high-altitude exercise, talk and laugh together, and yes—even pay our humble respects to the majestic wrath of a Rocky Mountain snowstorm.

I was actually enjoying myself. As we tramped and laughed our way down the mountain, I began to realize that the trip wasn't a failure; it was a smashing success.

We hadn't reached the summit, but we had enjoyed the attempt. We had given it our best shot. We enjoyed good fellowship and awesome surroundings. The destination was incidental—it was the journey itself that would make the trip a fond memory.

DESTINATION OR JOURNEY?

I wonder . . .

When it comes to our lives and careers, do you and I unknowingly make the same mistake of concentrating too intently on the mountaintop? Do we sometimes become so focused on an ultimate destination that we fail to enjoy the journey?

At work, without realizing it, we might not allow ourselves to think we're successful unless we achieve a certain job title or income level.

At home we might become so focused on our goal of turning the kids into responsible young adults that we fail to appreciate, encourage, and enjoy them today.

We might become so enthralled with a planned two-week vacation that our work and other responsibilities seem like bothersome distractions until then.

We may fantasize so much about a retirement lifestyle that the decades of labor between now and then become mere means to an end—not fulfilling experiences in themselves.

If we make the mountaintops our criteria for success, do we then consider ourselves failures during the long months and years we put in trying to reach those summits?

And what if circumstances do not grant us our mountaintops? Like Rocky Mountain storm clouds, most circumstances are beyond our personal control. Despite our best efforts, there is no guarantee we will reach our chosen summits.

WHAT'S YOUR PERSPECTIVE?

When you think about it, personal success seems to boil down to one key word: Perspective.

Perspective enables us to stand back from the mountain we are about to climb and appreciate not only the pinnacle, but also the pathway.

Perspective enables us to change our attitudes about the endeavor. Instead of thinking, *I'll succeed if I reach the top,* we'll think, *I may or may not make the top. But I'm going to give it all I've got, and I'm going to enjoy myself in the attempt.*

I've now climbed enough mountains to believe that success is not really whether we reach a destination, but how we handle the journey.

It is enjoying the moment. Seizing the day. Appreciating the now, not living just for the someday.

It is giving the endeavor our very best effort—today.

Stopping to delight in the view—today.
Building strong friendships—today.
Finding joy along the pathway—today.

Mountaintops can be exhilarating, but the summit is always a long way up. Only God knows whether we will reach it or whether storm clouds will turn us back.

But along the pathway, there is a beautiful world to see. Good fellowship to enjoy. Some lessons to learn.

So why not take a little more time?
And enjoy the journey?

TAKING ACTION

☐ What "mountaintops" do you tend to focus on in your pursuit of success in:
  your career?
  your marriage?
  your family?
  your finances?

☐ Take a pen and paper and list at least four practical ways you can help make sure you "enjoy the journey" en route to your mountaintops.

☐ In three sentences or less, write what personal success means to you. Then ask yourself: Does my definition stand up to the storm clouds? Will I be a success even if I don't reach the summit?

**From the man
in the ditch to
the corporate
president all of
us can learn …**

WILL ROGERS'S THREE SECRETS OF CAREER SUCCESS

*Nothing is work unless you would
rather be doing something else.*
WILLIAM JAMES

If you've ever stayed up late at
night and clicked through the
cable TV channels, you've seen
the success gurus crawling out of
the woodwork.

They buy thirty-minute blocks
of TV time and develop slick
shows with titles like "How to Get
Rich and Retire Next Week and
Be the Envy of Your Friends as
You Drive Your New Lamborghini
and Travel to Exotic Lands without Using Any of Your Own
Money, While You Sleep."

Of course, they don't reveal
their secret on TV. Instead, they
tell you that for just $395 (VISA
and MasterCard accepted), you
can own their amazing cassette-
tape home study program that
will bring you untold success and
happiness. Operators are standing by.

Success formulas are all around us. As part of my own professional development, I have attended business management classes and studied textbooks on human motivation and success. I've listened, pen in hand, as graduate professors and seminar leaders offered complex systems for maximum personal achievement.

On the job I have managed successful employees and have seen what it takes for people to succeed. I have also managed a few also-rans, observing what led to their mediocrity.

Through it all, one formula for success has stood out to me as probably the most profound of the lot— as well as the most practical. And it didn't come from a late-night cassette salesman, nor from a management Ph.D., nor from a textbook or seminar.

It came from a simple, rope-twirling cowboy, by the name of Will Rogers.

Those who have studied this man know that, beneath the wit and charm, Rogers was a wise observer of the human condition. He had a gentle way of entertaining audiences while shedding light on the truth.

Just a few weeks before his untimely death in 1935, this beloved American humorist addressed a businessmen's luncheon. In a room filled with men more schooled, trained, and qualified than he, Will Rogers observed:

M
A
N
T
A
L
K

> *If you want to be successful, it's just this simple: Know what you're doing. Love what you're doing. And believe in what you're doing. Yes, it's just that simple.*[1]

As you and I contemplate career success, we would be hard-pressed to find a business expert, seminar leader, or textbook author who has ever put it better.

KNOW WHAT YOU ARE DOING

It goes without saying that knowledge of one's field is vital to career success. And one of the fascinating joys of life is that no matter how much we study and learn, there is always more to discover.

Today, accumulated knowledge is everywhere at our fingertips. Libraries, universities, bookstores, seminars, public television, magazines, and computer networks offer an ever-expanding body of information that you and I can access to enhance our knowledge of practically any subject.

In the past, I have hired several people who came to me with good educational pedigrees and lots of potential. However, once they learned the basic skills of their jobs, they seemed to feel that their education was complete. They held their own for awhile, but as we took on new technology and entered new markets, they were soon left in the dust, somewhat perplexed that they weren't receiving the advancement they felt they deserved.

I've also had the privilege of managing employees who were dedicated to "knowing what they are doing." I'm blessed with such a team right now. One of my people, Jean, is sixty-five going on thirty. On her own, she has subscribed to newsletters that help her stay sharp on professional trends and job skills. When we upgraded computer systems she eagerly took the manuals home and learned the new systems on her home computer. She attended evening user's groups at her own initiative and came into the office the following day glowing with excitement at what she was learning.

Some people her age might think that it's too late to learn all this new stuff; this special lady can't seem to get enough. She is dedicated to knowing what she's doing, and it's a delight to have her on my team. Our company, and indeed our entire industry, is benefiting from her commitment.

Formal schooling may give us nice-sounding degrees, but people who know what they are doing make a personal commitment to learning their chosen fields inside and out. They study, experience, and learn from business cycles, market trends, and human nature. They keep up with the latest developments through trade publications, professional seminars, trade shows, and personal networking. All of this gives them "good instincts" for what works and what doesn't, thus making them invaluable to their organizations.

LOVE WHAT YOU ARE DOING

Most of us spend more than one-third of each weekday on the job—almost one-fourth of the total hours in a year.

That's a lot of time, so Will Rogers makes a lot of sense. If we're going to spend all that time working at our careers, why not enjoy ourselves? If we don't, we're merely plugging away on a dusty trail, longing desperately for mediocre mountaintops called "Friday" or "vacation" or "retirement." But if we love what we're doing, we'll "enjoy the journey," whether the trail is level and scenic or rough and stormy.

Loving what we do does not mean finding the perfect job with the perfect organization, for you and I know such a position doesn't exist. Rather, love for our work is a conscious choice we make every moment of every working day.

We can either roll out of bed muttering, "Good Lord, it's morning," or we can roll out saying, "Good morning, Lord!"

We can tell ourselves, "Just five days till Friday," or we can say, "I've got five whole days to make good things happen!"

We can moan, "Why me?" when an obstacle blocks our path, or we can say, "All right! This is what separates the men from the boys!"

We can say, "I'm working for a paycheck," or we can say, "I'm providing a service that makes a difference!"

It really is up to us. There are no horrible jobs, just horrible attitudes toward jobs.

Two men are digging a deep ditch, sweat pouring from their brows as they work with jackhammers and shovels. As you approach the first man, you hear him muttering an oath as he wrestles to loosen a rock.

"What are you doing?" you ask him.

"Digging a *!#&* ditch," he replies.

"What for?" you ask.

"For twelve *!#&* dollars an hour," he answers.

You approach the second man. As you draw near, you hear him humming a soft tune as he wrestles with his own rock.

"What are you doing?" you ask.

He looks up and smiles through heavy beads of perspiration. "I'm preparing the foundation," he replies.

"What for?"

"For a beautiful building," he says, stretching his arms upward. "It's going to provide office space for two hundred companies and thousands of workers."

Each man's labor is the same, but their perspectives are different. One sees only the dirt and the rocks and the Friday paycheck. The other sees a beautiful skyscraper and thousands of people enjoying the fruit of his labor. One brings self-pity to his work. The other brings passion.

Each has made his choice. Which man would you rather have working for you?

BELIEVE IN WHAT YOU ARE DOING

My sixty-five-year-old employee believes in what she is doing. So does the second man in the ditch. They both believe their small contribution is making a lasting difference, and this attitude is reflected in the quality of their work.

When you believe in what you are doing, you labor with integrity and purpose. Instead of watching the clock, you watch the quality of your output. You take on the mind-set that what you are doing is part of your unique mission in life.

Mission.

That word has regained its deserved popularity recently, for several studies of successful people have concluded that at the very foundation of their lives is a driving purpose—a "mission that matters." Our mission is not necessarily our occupation, for our life's purpose can and should transcend our jobs. But the more we are able to relate our work to our mission, the more we will believe in what we are doing.

It makes sense, then, that the worker who seems to shift into neutral and coast through his career has never really thought seriously about his personal mission. Instead of asking himself, "What difference will I make?" he asks, "How much money will I make?" He thinks short-term, not long-term; salary, not satisfaction.

The dedicated worker, on the other hand, is driven by the belief that his work is making a difference. His paycheck is only one benefit of his job, and even if he were financially independent he would probably continue working because the work is, to him, of long-range significance.

No one can select our missions for us. Parents can't. Bosses and peers can't. It's up to us, as we thoughtfully and prayerfully consider the aptitudes and desires God has created within us.

One strategy I suggest to audiences has proven helpful in thinking through one's personal mission in life. I call it the "20/20 Hindsight Test." You choose a quiet location and give yourself at least thirty minutes of thinking time. Imagine yourself at age ninety, looking back on your soon-to-be-completed life's journey. What three things would you most like to have accomplished? What would you want to have done that is of lasting significance? What important legacy do you want to leave for your children and grandchildren? See if you can write your answers in a series of one-sentence statements.

Then bring it back to the present. As you contemplate what you have written, some thoughts should begin to surface regarding your long-range purpose in life. Many men and women find it helpful to conclude the exercise by completing this statement: "I believe the mission I am created to fulfill during my time on earth is to: _____

_____

_____."

When you have a strong sense of personal mission and can relate your work to it, it's natural and easy to believe in what you are doing. And that belief naturally lends an extra dimension of dedication and fulfillment to your work.

If Will Rogers's mission was to lighten our burdens by getting us laughing and thinking, I believe he accomplished the mission with honors. The rope-twirling cowboy has now been gone for more than half a century, but even today his work continues to lift people's burdens. Truly he knew what he was doing . . . loved what he was doing . . . believed in what he was doing.

Do you?

TAKING ACTION

☐ *Imagine that you are managing an employee who obviously does not know, love, or believe in what he is doing. Describe his attitudes and work habits, and their effect on his fellow employees. Do any of these traits describe your own attitudes and work habits?*

☐ *What are three specific things you would like to do during the next year to enrich your knowledge of your vocational field? When will you do them?*

☐ *Go through the "20/20 Hindsight Test." What do you believe is your personal "mission that matters"? In what way(s) does your present work relate to it?*

M
A
N
T
A
L
K

How to achieve
a worthwhile
dream

THE
ACHIEVEMENT
PROGRESSION

The poorest of all men is not the man without a cent but the man without a dream.
SOURCE UNKNOWN

In 1989 Robin Williams starred in a fascinating motion picture titled *Dead Poets Society.* Williams played the role of John Keating, a new literature instructor in a prestigious (i.e., stuffy) north-eastern boy's academy.

But this teacher was like a pair of neon orange running shoes at a black-tie affair. To him, life was to be lived with creative passion, not lock-step mediocrity. So Keating dedicated himself to helping his students discover and achieve their life's potential.

On the first day of class, the new teacher took his students into the foyer, where the walls were filled with photographs of the classes of boys who had grad-uated decades before. Like those boys in Keating's class, each of the hundreds of boys in the photographs had once been young and carefree. Each had thought he would live forever. But now they were all gone . . . deceased . . . mere memories on the wall of a classroom building.

As Keating's students gaped at one photograph after another of young men who had thought they would live forever, they began to realize that they, too, would someday be gone from this earth, that life was just a brief moment of eternity. Their mouths hung open in wonder as their teacher stood behind them and whispered:

Seize the day . . . make your lives extraordinary.

In the packed theater where Kathy and I saw the movie, you could have heard a pin drop. The scene moved us all, and the words burned a place in my memory. Seize the day . . . make your lives extraordinary.

Much as we would like to think we'll live forever, the truth is that we spend just a few short years on earth. One New Testament writer described human life as a "vapor." The psalmist wrote to God that:

You speak, and man turns back to dust. . . . We glide along the tides of time as swiftly as a racing river, and vanish as quickly as a dream. Psalm 90:3, 5-6, TLB

BACK TO THE FUTURE

In the last chapter we described the "20/20 Hindsight Test" as one way to help determine our mission in life. There is a hidden benefit to this exercise as well. In addition to helping us decide on our life purpose, the exercise can help us discover an area or two in which we have not yet "seized the day" and lived up to the potential God gave us.

So take a moment to imagine again that you are age ninety, looking back over the years of your life. This time, instead of thinking from a positive perspective (what you feel best about having accomplished by age ninety), evaluate your life from the negative side:

Do you have any regrets?

Anything you wish you had applied more energy to?

An opportunity you let pass by?

It could be that you never took that shot at opening your own business, although you thought about it all your life.

Maybe you wish you had followed your dream of going back to school, getting a graduate degree. Or launching into a new vocational field.

You may wish you had spent less energy at the job and more energy nurturing a friendship.

Or more energy drawing closer to your children.

Maybe you felt led to begin a concerted effort to meet a community or worldwide need, but you never acted on it.

You may wish you had read more great books. Studied and memorized more of the Bible.

Or taken that dream trip.

Whatever you come up with, the obvious advantage of this exercise is that it's imaginary; you can quickly bring yourself back to the present, shift direction, and set out to accomplish some of the elusive desires of your heart. For a few moments you placed yourself among the boys in the photographs on the wall, but now you're among the young boys staring at the photographs, realizing there is still time to make a difference.

For those who actually are near the end of their lives, the story might be sadder. Any regrets they feel are real—and time and energy may not allow for dramatic life-style changes. Indeed, surveys have shown that a common lament among older senior citizens goes something like this:

"I wish I had used my time better . . . "

"I wish I had taken more chances . . . "

"I wish I had pursued my dreams . . . "

"I wish . . . "

The psalmist acknowledged the shortness of our lifespan when he wrote to God, "Teach us to number our days and recognize how few they are; help us to spend them as we should" (Psalm 90:12, TLB).

How about you? Are you "seizing the day"? Are there dreams and desires hidden deep inside that may not be getting a fair chance because of the fear of failure, lack of money, procrastination, or misplaced priorities?

BRINGING YOUR DREAM TO REALITY

As an avid observer and participant in life, I have noticed that those of us who manage to latch onto a dream and see it through to fulfillment are not necessarily more gifted or fortunate than others; just more determined. In fact, whether we realize it or not, those who achieve a special desire almost always go through a sequence of eight specific steps to bring a dream to reality.

This sequence is summarized in the following diagram. I call it "The Achievement Progression" because each step naturally leads into the next as we progress toward the attainment of a worthwhile dream. I share it with you not as a rigid set of rules to follow, but as a series of suggested steps which can help all of us better "seize the day . . . and make our lives extraordinary."

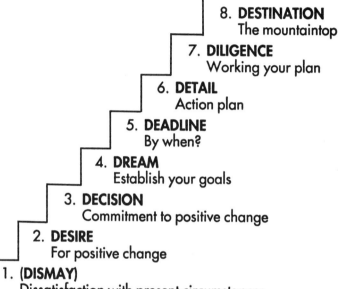

8. **DESTINATION**
The mountaintop

7. **DILIGENCE**
Working your plan

6. **DETAIL**
Action plan

5. **DEADLINE**
By when?

4. **DREAM**
Establish your goals

3. **DECISION**
Commitment to positive change

2. **DESIRE**
For positive change

1. **(DISMAY)**
Dissatisfaction with present circumstances

THE ACHIEVEMENT PROGRESSION

To help you put the Achievement Progression to work, let's take a "Busy Man's Tour" through the eight steps to define them and observe how they might work in a real-life scenario we can probably all identify with.

THE SOFT TRUTH

Here's the setting for our example: You've reached middle age, when your broad mind and narrow waist have begun trading places. You know you need to lose weight, tone up your muscles and get back in good cardiovascular shape. Your two sons, Alas and

Alack, run circles around you on the basketball court. Instead of seizing the day, you seize the potato chips. Your idea of an exciting night alone with your wife is falling asleep in front of the TV. You get the idea.

But for the past several months or years you've just been too busy to do much about it. With everything you've got going, you've been too tired or, well, too lazy.

But you want to change that, and here's where the Achievement Progression will help you. As we walk through it and apply it to one's quest for better physical fitness, you'll find that the progression makes a lot of sense for helping us achieve our other dreams as well.

THE ACHIEVEMENT PROGRESSION
STEP 1. (DISMAY)

This first step is in parentheses because it is not always necessary for one to be dismayed with his present circumstances to start moving toward greater things. However, as in our physical fitness scenario, dismay is often the initial motivator. The man who knows he can and should be a better "keeper of the temple" may need to start with a sense of personal disgust over the life-style choices that have led to his present condition. Dismay sounds like this: "I'm sick of being out of shape. Tired of being tired. I've let myself go too long."

STEP 2. DESIRE

Without a desire for change, of course, no action toward positive change is possible. We know that people with addictions to drugs, alcohol, or nicotine can rarely be helped if they do not confess a strong inner desire to be cured. The desire cannot come from someone else such as a concerned parent, spouse, or child—it must be owned and believed by the person needing to change. Likewise, for a person to achieve greater physical fitness or some other worthwhile goal, he must first own a strong inner desire for positive change in his life. During this step, we hear ourselves saying, "I want to change. I want to get back in shape."

STEP 3. DECISION
While Dismay says, "I'm sick of being out of shape," and Desire says, "I want to get back in shape," Decision says, "I will get back in shape." This is the step in which we decide that we're no longer going to settle for mediocrity—we're making a commitment to positive change.

STEP 4. DREAM
Robert Schuller asks, "What great thing would you attempt if you knew you could not fail?" The Dream step is the act of thinking big (or in our scenario, thinking small) to clarify what exactly it is we want to accomplish. The Dream step might sound like this:

"I want my cholesterol level to be well below 200."
"I want my blood pressure to be right around 120/80."
"I want my waistline to be two inches slimmer."
"I want to feel stronger and firmer."
"I want to be able to work and play with greater energy and endurance."

STEP 5. DEADLINE
Someone has aptly said that a goal is a dream with a deadline. Deadlines are vital, for they hold us accountable and motivate us to keep going in order to meet an upcoming rendezvous with time. I know

that I'm always more diligent with my running when I've registered for an upcoming road race—if I decreased my runs between races to two or three miles, the knowledge that I have just a few weeks to build back up to 6.2-mile shape motivates me to lace up those shoes and hit the road in the early morning. In the Deadline step, we get specific as to when we want to see our dream accomplished. It's important to be realistic, but at the same time create just enough urgency to keep us on track. For example, we might look over our Dreams and say, "I will accomplish these dreams six months from today, starting now."

STEP 6. DETAIL

This step involves formulating a specific plan of action with measurable checkpoints to keep you progressing toward your dream. For example:

"I will begin tonight with twenty push-ups and add one each evening until I can do seventy-five. I will also begin with twenty bent-leg sit-ups and add at the same pace until I can do seventy-five."

"I will begin tomorrow morning with a brisk fifteen-minute walk and add both speed and distance during the following weeks. Within a month I'll do a combination walk-jog, then build up to a complete jog, until I can comfortably run three miles or thirty minutes without stopping."

"Beginning tonight I will reduce salt intake by not adding salt at the table or while cooking."

"Beginning tonight I will reduce saturated fat intake by drinking skim milk, limiting red meat to extra lean and only twice per week (increasing consumption of fish and poultry), and cutting back on high-fat desserts."

We'll take a more thorough look at effective goal

planning when we talk about financial success. But this gives you the picture: the big dream, a specific time-frame, a detailed action plan.

STEP 7. DILIGENCE
This is where the talking and planning stop and the action starts. Diligence is:

Pulling yourself out of bed thirty minutes earlier and taking those first groggy steps out the door for the morning walk.

Stopping after one cookie instead of the usual five.

Getting down on the bedroom floor for those push-ups and sit-ups, and doing five more when you feel your muscles are ready to burst, especially when you don't feel like it. And trust me, there will be plenty of those times. Diligence is needed to overcome the inevitable discouragements and defeats along the way. It's discipline, perseverance, all those Vince Lombardi–type words. But you'll also experience lots of victories and encouragements. There's a special rush of vitality when you start to feel yourself getting into shape. You sense the old strength and energy returning. You rejoice when you can tighten your belt buckle another notch. You notice that you're more effective at work and at play because your heart is pumping oxygen-filled blood to your brain, muscles, and other organs with greater efficiency.

STEP 8. DESTINATION
This is the mountaintop! You've lost some ton-nage around your waist and your muscles have bet-ter strength and tone. More importantly, the cholesterol and blood pressure levels have improved, and you look and feel better. You can give your boys a good game on the basketball court, and

an exciting evening alone with your wife takes on a whole new meaning. (But we'll talk about that later in the book. Stay in shape for it.)

A fair warning is in order here: The Destination stage can be a double-edged sword. Yes, reaching the mountaintop can be a thrilling accomplishment, a proud memory worth cherishing. But the thrill can be fleeting, and after a few days of celebration the adrenaline will diminish and you'll be ready to launch out after your next challenge. Sometimes, especially if we choose our dreams unwisely, Destination is spelled D-i-s-a-p-p-o-i-n-t-m-e-n-t. Like the man who said, "I spent twenty years climbing to the top of the ladder, only to realize that the ladder was leaning against the wrong house." This man had chosen a dream called "Money = Happiness." When he reached his destination he found there was still a big empty vacuum inside him because his achievement had been at the expense of his wife, children, extended family, and friends. Even some very worthwhile dreams bring only temporary satisfaction. That's okay. We can't expect everything we do to change the world, but we can put everything we've got into our days so that, when we really do reach age ninety, we can look back with satisfaction on a life well lived.

WHAT'S YOUR DREAM?

Now it's time to take your personal dream and walk it through the eight-step sequence. You might be thinking of a career move, a volunteer effort in your church or city, or a special dream you have for your home and family.

Whatever your dream may be, if you are confident that it is worthwhile in light of your short span of time on this planet, don't let the dream stagnate and die inside you. With God's guidance, and with the help of the Achievement Progression . . .

Seize the day . . . make your life extraordinary.

TAKING ACTION

☐ *If you knew your life would end in one hour and you were looking back, what regrets, if any, would you have? What missed opportunities would stand out to you?*

☐ *What does the advice to "seize the day . . . make your life extraordinary" mean to you personally?*

☐ *Do you have a special dream you've been holding deep inside? What is it? In your imagination, walk it through the Achievement Progression. Does it feel like a dream you should pursue in real life?*

> Effective time management can help you enjoy the journey.

GETTING IT
ALL DONE

For everything there is a season, and a time for every matter under heaven.

SOLOMON (Ecclesiastes 3:1; RSV)

Job.
Personal dreams.
Wife.
Children.
Friends.
Finances.
Time alone.
Time with God.

Every day multiple activities and demands clamor for our time and attention.

We've heard, and may agree with, the personal priority structure that places God first, family next, job last. But let's face it—most of the time our jobs clamor the loudest, consuming at least ten hours of each weekday plus the inevitable evening and weekend "think" time.

In other words, the best hours and energy levels of our week are taken up by only one of our priorities. The other important activities of life must be squeezed in around that big chunk of core time devoted to our jobs.

IF WE THINK WE'VE GOT IT TOUGH . . .

Lest we feel too sorry for ourselves, it's important to note that in many marriages the working wife carries an even bigger load. Most of us men would have to confess that we tend to consider ourselves done for the day when we arrive home. We've put in our eight to ten hours so we deserve to unwind. But when our dear wives return home from their workplace, they start right in on their second job. We sit and read the paper; they go to work in the kitchen. We consume dinner and retreat to our evening activities or TV; they clean the kitchen and begin household chores, all the while serving as chief referee, cab driver, and answering service for the children.

I'm sorry to admit that the generation in which I grew up thought this division of labor was rather normal, a carryover from the days of Ward and June Cleaver. Those of us who consider ourselves enlightened have had to make a conscious effort to change the norms that led to such an unbalanced workload at home.

But while sharing the home duties with our wives might make things a bit fairer, it also adds to our list of things to do.

Getting it all done can be tough.

SERVE TIME, OR LET TIME SERVE YOU

My generation also assigned great virtue, and distinctive manhood, to the rush. If we were *extremely busy*, we must be *important*. We were working on *something big*; therefore, we were *responsible, successful people*.

But just a few years after I entered the work force some startling discoveries began to surface. The medical profession began calling the harried work ethic "Type-A Behavior," revealing that men and women who lived by this code were prone to high blood pressure, heart disease, strokes, and other debilitating illnesses.

Psychologists joined in, proclaiming that being so intensely focused on work and other activities could actually lead to a loss of effectiveness and fighting spirit. They called it "burnout."

Observant businessmen began to admit that overwork could actually be destructive. A former chairman of Inland Steel sounded the alarm when he wrote, "[The overworked executive] is overworked because he wants to be. And frequently, the longer and harder he works, the less effective he becomes.... Pity him, but recognize him for the dangerous liability that he is."[1]

In the 1990s we now know that the Type-A lifestyle is counter-productive—unfair to our families, employers, and ourselves. So when we focus on getting things done, we are not talking about taking on more hypertension through longer, harder hours. Instead, we're talking about learning to make wise choices—working smarter, not harder.

We can either serve time or let it serve us. If we harness the minutes and hours to get important things done more efficiently, we'll also discover the time to stop and smell some roses along the way:

to look, and perhaps see for the first time;

to listen, and hear what God and our loved ones are telling us;

to smell, touch, and taste a creation still waiting to be fully discovered.

Indeed, smart time management can help us achieve our mission in life as well as our special dreams . . . while helping us "enjoy the journey."

Is there a long "things to do" list hounding at you?

Are you feeling that you could be more effective if only you had more time?

Have you felt frustrated that you aren't able to spend as much time with your children as you would like?

Have you ever heard yourself asking, "How am I ever going to get it all done?"

I wish I could tell you that I have mastered the challenge of personal time management, that I accomplish every single thing I set out to do. But I can't. Because of the way real life works, making the best of my time is a moment-by-moment battle.

But, of necessity, I've worked hard at it—and learned a few things to help me make better choices, get more done more effectively, and enjoy the journey. If you would like to be more effective in getting things done, thinking through these ideas may be a smart investment of your time today.

TEN STEPS TO GETTING THINGS DONE

1. *Recognize the activities that have been consuming your time.* Ask your wife or a close friend to help you determine which activities have been monopolizing your time in recent weeks. Among the most common time consumers:

___TV
___Inability to say no
___The job
___Daydreaming

___Worry
___Meetings
___Phone calls
___Piles of papers
___Hobbies
___Committees
___Relatives
___Other activities

2. *Review your life priorities.* When I was in college, an older friend of mine who was a real success in the business world shared the order of personal priorities he tried to live by:

A. My relationship with God.
B. My relationship with my wife.
C. My relationship with my children.
D. My personal mission (interrelated with A, B, C, and E.)
E. My business's well-being.

His list had ten items on it, including friendships, personal health and financial freedom. But you get the idea. It worked beautifully for him, even though he shared the common dilemma of having to give a disproportionate number of hours to his business.

Your personal priorities will vary depending on your values and circumstances. The important thing is that you give careful thought to those things that are most significant to you in the long run.

Here again, the "20/20 Hindsight Test" might be of help. If you imagine yourself at age ninety, looking back on your life, what personal priorities will most make you feel that your life has been worthwhile and meaningful? Write them down in order of long-range significance.

Now come back to the present. Are the activities to which you have been devoting most of your time a good indication of your life priorities? (You may find it helpful to ask these questions from two perspectives: your on-the-job time as well as your personal time.)

3. *List all the things that need to be done.* Write them down—the big things, the little things. What's on your mind? Don't leave anything out.

4. *Delete non-priority items.* This step is especially important if you have become swamped with tasks and responsibilities. Take your list of things to do and for each item ask: "In light of my life priorities, is this task really that important right now?" Will working on it mean cheating a higher priority? Then chances are you will want to delete this lower priority from your list.

Sometimes this step involves a humbling but necessary procedure called "backing out gracefully." You know you've reached this point when, after two or three consecutive months of saying, "Why sure, I'd be glad to," your inner voice tells you, *I'm going to sell the house and the kids and move to Tahiti.*

You know the feeling. Overcommitted. Little control of your time or your life. Doing so many things at once that you can't give any one of them your best effort. Feeling like one unbalanced, worn-out, Type-A individual.

First you have to admit to yourself that in accepting new opportunities, you did not fully consider your priorities or commitments. Then comes the hard part—going to those who asked you to serve, admitting that you've taken on too many things to be effective, and asking to be relieved of the responsibility.

None of us like to do this, for we believe in keeping

our commitments. But if you find you have gotten carried away with favors for people at the expense of your priorities, don't be afraid to "back out gracefully." Doing so may be the best favor you could do for that person or committee because now they will be able to replace you with someone who can devote more attention to the endeavor.

5. *Rank the remaining items in the order of importance.* Are there tasks which just can't wait any longer? Place the letter *A* beside each of these items to rank them as top priority. Place a *B* beside those that need to be done as soon as possible, and a *C* beside those that are not as important.

Now take another few moments to go back through each letter grouping, ranking each item again in order of importance: *A*-1, *A*-2, *A*-3, and so on.

You now know which items are top priority (the *A* group) and in what order you should work on those items in your top group. This procedure will prevent you from spending time today on low-priority items while very important ones stand waiting.

6. *Delegate tasks if possible.* This does not mean to dump your responsibilities on another person simply because you don't wish to do them. To delegate is simply to admit that there may be someone either better qualified or with more time for the task than you.

If you have a secretary, for example, it would be a foolish waste of time for you to struggle at typing a business letter or report. She is trained for that sort of thing, and it's just good business to delegate a typing project to her. Likewise, your teen-age son may be handy at household repairs. If you're having a rough time getting around to installing the utility shelves, challenge your son with the task. Let him in on how you are trying to make the best use of your time—it will also be a good learning experience for him.

7. *Determine which items can be done as husband-and-wife or family projects.* Are you changing the oil in the Oldsmobile this weekend? Maybe now's the time to teach Mike and Jimmy how to do it themselves. Or if you're finally going to refinish the antique cabinet, why not make a date with your wife to work at it together?

Household projects can be fun. One dad I know has perfected the art of holding family work mornings. As each family member rakes leaves, washes windows, or weeds flower beds, he goes from one to another and works alongside for fifteen minutes or so. He uses the time to talk with each child about school, sports, boyfriends, or girlfriends. Then, before he moves on to help the next person, he says something like, "You know, I really love you, and I'm glad you're my son [or daughter]. Thanks for being such a big help today." At the end of the day, projects completed, the family votes on a special treat: a pizza feast, movies, miniature golf, or some other celebration of a day's work well done.

8. *Schedule the items on monthly and weekly calendars.* Scheduling is one of your best investments of time, for fifteen minutes of advance planning can be worth hours later on. A monthly calendar will help you see thirty days in advance the basic chunks of time that will be needed for given tasks. Using a pencil to allow for changes, schedule your month according to the groupings and numerical priorities you've assigned to each item.

When you have an overview of what the next

month holds, you'll want to be more specific. "When on the twenty-second or twenty-third of this month will I make the time to write my speech? What hours on Saturday mornings will I block out for recreation with the kids?" To answer these questions, you'll find it helpful to use a pocket calendar that shows a full week at a time and allows plenty of space for each day's events.

You can get as specific as you like when it comes to filling in your weekly calendar. First, you might schedule in those things that are or should be regular experiences: family activities, church commitments, office time, exercise time, etc. Then, using your monthly calendar for reference, determine which days of the week and which times of the day will be best for your prioritized activities.

9. *Follow through with your planning.* Each evening, take ten minutes to refine your schedule for the following day. This will help you focus on your top priorities first thing in the morning.

If necessary, gently tell coworkers or family members that you must concentrate on some important work, and ask them to hold visits or phone calls. Then begin the first task on your day's calendar and try to stay with it until it is completed.

Time management specialists often recommend that we do our most dreaded job first during the day. For example, Matilda the Hun is an unhappy client. It's your job to keep her happy, so you know you must call her and try to make peace. Your natural tendency might be to put that call last on your schedule and then breathe a sigh of relief at the end of the day when other events have preempted your phone call. This only gets Matilda more steamed at your company because you didn't call, so you'll face even greater wrath tomorrow.

But if you call her first thing today, you'll be able to cross the task off your list. You'll feel better because you made a client feel good (or at least tried), and you'll have some positive momentum for the other challenges of your day.

Sometimes it helps to devise little rewards for yourself. "After two more phone calls, then I'll go get a cup of coffee." "After I've completed this tax form, we'll go get a frozen yogurt." And sometimes the only reward necessary is the sheer delight of crossing an item off your schedule as "Done."

10. *Learn to say no—graciously.* "Dan! We have an urgent project that's in trouble. It's due in two weeks, and we can't think of a better man than you to help us."

"Dan! The chairman of the finance committee at church just got transferred to Nome, Alaska. We really need a man of your financial savvy to head up the team during the next two years."

"Dan! I was supposed to attend the meeting this afternoon, but my wife needs a ride to her Guns and Ammo Club meeting. Can you sit in for me?"

As you seek to make the best of your time, you can count on a tidal wave of urgent and flattering requests.

Someone once asked former president Dwight D. Eisenhower how he managed to sort through all the demands on his time. Eisenhower replied: "I had to learn to distinguish the urgent from the important."

Perhaps Ike's wisdom can help us in deciding whether to say yes or no to all the temptations that come our way. From experience, I have learned that most things labeled "Urgent" are usually the result of poor planning and should be handled with caution.

And even if the request can be considered "Important," I have to weigh it against my life priorities and present commitments. If time allows and I'm ready for a new challenge—great! But if my schedule is full and the opportunity does not mesh with my priorities, I must say no. Which is never easy, for our culture has conditioned us to feel guilty when we must turn someone down.

My friend Steve Douglass, with whom I recently coauthored *The One-Percent Edge: 15 Minutes a Day to Personal Excellence*, suggests a great way of saying no graciously: "I would love to . . . but I can't." It is as simple as that. Say it with a smile in your voice and a word of appreciation for being asked. See if you can help the solicitor think of an alternative solution to his problem. But don't make his problem yours.

NOW GIVE IT A TRY

People who are already wise stewards of their time do most of the above naturally, without really thinking about it.

But if you are among those who could manage time better, give these ten steps a try. The process may seem laborious at first, but it will pay huge dividends if you follow through and don't give up. Indeed, smart time management is not meant to imprison us to laborious routine, but to help us choose the important over the urgent, the priorities over the non-priorities.

Done wisely, it can actually free us from routine, and give us more hours to better enjoy the time of our life.

TAKING ACTION

☐ *With pad and pen in hand, think through the ongoing activities and dimensions of your life. Rank them in order of personal priority, 1 through 10.*

☐ *In light of your personal priorities, what are the three biggest time-wasters in your life?*

☐ *Within the next week, obtain both a monthly and weekly calendar and work through the remaining steps suggested in this chapter.*

Solomon's formula for personal problem solving

THE WISDOM PROGRESSION

Q: *Tell me, Old-Timer, where did you get your good judgment?*
A: *From experience.*
Q: *And where did you get your experience?*
A: *From bad judgment.*

You're at your desk at work, minding your own business, when an important client calls. He thinks he's been mistreated by your company. In reality, he's a prima donna—rude, arrogant, demanding. What do you say to him?

You have the opportunity to buy the kind of house you have always wanted. It's perfect. But the fancier neighborhood, extra floor space, and built-in spa would more than double your monthly house payments. Should you go ahead with the deal?

In the past few months, you've sensed a wall going up between you and your teenage son. His grades have slipped, he's missed curfews, and now he's challenging you: "Da-a-a-d, I told you—it's *Friday the 13th, Part 27* at the drive-in. Todd's driving—his folks say it's okay. I'm going!" In addition to your convictions about twenty-seven-part slasher movies, you know how Todd drives, who else he's likely to pick up along the way, and what substances he's likely to carry with him in the glove compartment and trunk of his car. What do you do?

Perhaps you've faced situations like these recently. And probably some much tougher ones. Whether we like it or not, problems, questions, and tough decisions are an inescapable part of a man's world.

The way we go about such decisions can have a dramatic impact on ourselves and our loved ones. A justifiably angry response could lose a client as well as our boss's favor. One financial mistake could wipe out cash reserves or tie up future earnings for years. The wrong action with our teenagers could separate us further from them while a lack of action could ruin their lives.

Every day, in every part of life, we need wisdom.

M
A
N
T
A
L
K

As I grow older, this word becomes more and more significant to me. In my growing-up years, "wisdom" was something remote—an intangible concept that didn't seem to have much to do with real life. I thought a wise person was always a white-haired sage with a witty, penetrating saying for every occasion—like "wise old Ben Franklin" or a "wise old grandfather."

It didn't cross my mind that I could obtain wisdom, or that I'd even want to—especially before I retired. I thought you're either born with it or that it suddenly strikes you someday while you're rocking away on the front porch. Obviously, I didn't fit either category.

But I wanted to be successful, in my career as well as my relationships, so I went after knowledge with a passion. Gathered all the good grades I could. Passed all the exams. Behaved just enough to maintain a good record in that hallowed document known as "The Cumulative File." In school, being "smart" had more appeal than being "wise" anyway . . . as long as we didn't sit in the front row with the nerds or ruin the grading curve for football players like Hammerhead Sagurski.

Then a funny thing happened on the way to real life. In the years since I passed all those exams, at least 95 percent of the names, dates, facts, and figures I learned have drifted out through my ears and right up through the hole in the ozone layer. The stellar Cumulative File I worked so hard to build has probably been recycled into an eight-roll Valu-Pac. I wasn't long out of school before I realized something important: Education had given me all kinds of temporary knowledge, but real-life problems go far beyond who won the Battle of Bunker Hill or how to separate subject from predicate.

Life's problems demand wisdom.

Every time I found myself asking, "What on earth should I do?" I needed to be wise, not just smart.

I needed to know how to apply knowledge in order to make the best possible decisions. I needed deeper insights into the problems I faced and a sound method for thinking them through.

THE WISDOM PROGRESSION

Proverbs, written primarily by Solomon, could well be called "The Wisest Man in the World Speaks Out on Success." If you ever want the short course on success, devour Proverbs. In this timeless collection of maxims for living, Solomon shares how we—yes, you and I—can exercise wisdom in the times of our life.

It's interesting to me how in many cases Solomon surrounds the word *wisdom* with three distinct nouns: *knowledge, understanding,* and *discretion* (or *discernment*). I believe these nouns provide the dynamic synergy that can help us make wiser choices and decisions throughout our lives.

KNOWLEDGE

Knowledge is the mind's filing system of trivia we've learned through schooling, reading, conversations, media, and experience. Knowledge is essential to wisdom, but it is not sufficient in itself. If one strives for knowledge only, he is like a personal computer without a program—without some type of ongoing evaluation-manipulation process, the knowledge will only lie useless.

UNDERSTANDING

Understanding is the mind's process of evaluating knowledge. Usually, the facts are weighed in light of personal experience, personal values, or the observed experiences of others. Understanding asks, "What will happen if I choose this option?" and replies as honestly and objectively as possible.

DISCRETION

Discretion is the moment of decision—the action phase of the wisdom progression. Discretion is the ability to make the best choice from among two or more alternatives, based on our evaluation (understanding) of each option's strengths and weaknesses.

GOING UPTOWN

Sometimes without knowing it, we actually go through this three-stage progression whenever we're called upon to make a decision. To illustrate, let's assume you need to go to town, and you're trying to decide whether to drive or walk. The process might go something like this:

Knowledge: I have to go to town. Town is five miles away. I can drive. Or I can walk.

Understanding: But five miles is five miles! Walking would take me three or more hours round-trip. Driving might take fifteen to thirty minutes. I don't have three hours.

Discretion: I will take the car.

In this oversimplified example, we can see how important each stage of the process is to the following stage. Without the proper facts (*knowledge*) your evaluation of the facts (*understanding*) would not have been able to compare driving time with walking time. Had you left out the *understanding* stage, you might have taken off on a three-hour hike with only thirty minutes in which to do it. And without the moment of decision (*discretion*), you'd still be standing there wondering what to do.

Now we can see why many of our older population are indeed wiser than the younger generation. Their years have often blessed them with a broader base of knowledge, more personal experience to guide their level of understanding, and more opportunities to practice and learn from their decisions (discretion). The old-timer at the beginning of this chapter had not suddenly been zapped with a bolt of wisdom when he came of age; instead, he became wise by learning from all the experiences of his life.

ROOM FOR ERROR

It makes sense, then, that wisdom happens if all three stages are employed at peak efficiency. Maximum knowledge of the situation, its related facts, its options. Thorough evaluation of that knowledge. A firm decision, based on the evaluation.

But like a chain, the progression can only be as strong as its weakest link.

Which leaves lots of room for error, doesn't it?

Yes, we need to take in all the knowledge we can. And we have a responsibility to set things down and analyze them through the best of human logic. But quite often even the best resources available are not enough to steer our minds to the right conclusion.

THE SOLID STARTING POINT

The wisest man in the world recognized that even he needed more than just a good dose of knowledge, understanding, and discretion in order to be wise. Solomon felt that no matter how smart he might be, every man needs a solid, inerrant starting point from which to begin every fact → evaluation → decision process. In Proverbs he wasted little time identifying that starting point for us:

*"I want to make the simple-minded wise! . . . I want those already wise to become the wiser and become leaders by exploring the depths of meaning in these nuggets of truth." How does a man become wise? **The first step is to trust and reverence the Lord!** (Proverbs 1:4-9, TLB, emphasis added)

Trust and reverence the Lord. As we wrestle with the constant stream of choices and decisions that flow our way, Solomon pointed us to a hearty, personal, day-by-day faith in God as the solid starting point in the Wisdom Progression.

Elsewhere in the Scriptures we are assured that God actually desires to give us wisdom. In James's very straightforward New Testament letter, we read: "If any of you lacks wisdom, he should ask God, who gives generously to all without finding fault, and it will be given to him" (James 1:5, NIV).

Solomon's own life illustrated the validity of this starting point. As detailed in Old Testament history, whenever Solomon gave God first place in his life his subsequent *knowledge* → *understanding* → *discretion* process yielded wise decisions. But if he put his own ego first and left God out of the progression, Solomon's human limitations yielded poor choices for which he and the entire nation of Israel suffered.

Solomon counsels us from hard-learned experience when he writes, "Don't ever trust yourself. In everything you do, *put God first,* and he will direct you and crown your efforts with success" (Proverbs 3:5-6, TLB, emphasis added).

Thus Solomon adds a crucial step at the beginning of the process to give us a four-stage progression:

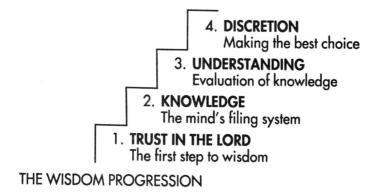

4. DISCRETION
Making the best choice

3. UNDERSTANDING
Evaluation of knowledge

2. KNOWLEDGE
The mind's filing system

1. TRUST IN THE LORD
The first step to wisdom

THE WISDOM PROGRESSION

PUTTING THE WISDOM PROGRESSION TO WORK

Is Solomon's Wisdom Progression practical today?

Well, why don't we try it out? What's on your mind right now? It could be a financial problem. A family dilemma. A marketing or personnel decision at work. On a sheet of paper, state the problem as clearly as you can. Then begin to adapt Solomon's formula to your situation by focusing for a few moments on the important starting point.

STEP 1. TRUST IN THE LORD

The natural tendency we all have is to either leave God out of the sequence entirely, or to reverse the Wisdom Progression and place God at the very end.

We'll wrestle the problem through and then ask God to bless our plans. Or if it becomes evident that we really blew our decision, we'll go running to him to bail us out.

We'd save ourselves a heap of trouble if we'd follow Solomon's advice to *begin at the starting point*—to trust and reverence the Lord God by giving him first place in our lives and by seeking to honor him in everything we do. If we are living for him, it follows that we will go to him with our problems—first, not last. (Just ask him for wisdom, James reminds us.)

In prayer, we may sense his special guidance. In his Word we may find the answer we need, spelled out for us in black and white.

Or, God just might want us to exercise the minds he's given us. That's where the Wisdom Progression comes in.

Begin by thanking God for the problem. While it may cause some pains now, God will use it to help you grow into a wiser, better person: "In all things

God works for the good of those who love him"
(Romans 8:28, NIV).

Then, ask for the Lord's guidance—that he would
clear your mind of all misleading thoughts, tangents,
or temptations to settle for less than the best.

STEP 2. KNOWLEDGE

When you've stated the problem as specifically
as possible and sought God's will, you're ready to
begin listing all possible courses of action.

This brainstorming process can be an especially
meaningful experience with a team of colleagues. At
work or church, round up several like-minded men
and women to help. For a family situation, team up
as husband and wife or as a family.

Don't be picky at this point. Write down every
idea, no matter how wild or impractical it may
sound. Often, an outlandish proposal plants the seed
for a practical one. For now, go for quantity, not quality. When many options are listed, chances of coming upon the best one are increased.

When you feel you've listed all possible options,
you're ready for step three.

STEP 3. UNDERSTANDING

Now's the time to be honest about every possible solution you've listed. Several can probably be
junked right away. The others, though, deserve careful evaluation in light of some serious questions:

a. Is this option in harmony with God's Word? (If
you cannot answer this question, search the Scriptures with a concordance or topical Bible, or consult
your pastor.)

b. Is this option a violation of civil law or my personal ethics?

c. Is this choice in line with my/our personal mission and priorities?

d. Do the pluses outweigh the minuses? (Make a pro-con list for each serious option. Under "pro," list every advantage you can think of. Under "con," every disadvantage or risk. Which side outweighs the other?)

e. What will be the long-range effect of this choice? (Imagine yourself five years from now, looking back. Are you glad you made the decision you did? Why or why not?)

These questions, and any others that weigh heavily on your mind, will help you narrow your list of alternatives to the two or three most viable.

STEP 4. DISCRETION

After weighing the alternatives, and perhaps thinking, talking, and praying further on them, make your decision. Choose the course of action that stands up best to your evaluation questions. Then begin putting your solution into action.

As an act of trust, thank God for his guidance and commit the situation to him. Then get on with life, confident that you have made the wisest choice possible.

TAKING ACTION

☐ *Think of a recent "bad" decision made by you or an acquaintance. In retrospect, which stage of the Wisdom Progression do you think was inappropriately applied?*

☐ *Name one decision you face right now. Within the next twenty-four hours, take your problem through the Wisdom Progression.*

☐ *During the next month, read one chapter per day of Proverbs, highlighting principles that are especially meaningful to you.*

PART TWO

Making the Most of Your Money

The common denominators of financial success

THE JOY OF FINANCIAL FREEDOM

There was a time when a fool and his money were soon parted, but now it happens to everybody.
ADLAI STEVENSON

Jeff and MaryAnn were typical of the couples I worked with while serving as senior consultant for a financial planning firm. Their combined income was far above average, and they hadn't encountered any devastating setbacks. Yet, financially, they were barely keeping their heads above water.

"It seems like we should have more to show for all our hard work," Jeff said during our initial meeting. "But as you can see, our monthly expenses consume just about everything."

"We'd really like to be putting some aside for retirement and for the kids' college education," MaryAnn joined in. "Really, we just need some breathing room. But with all our monthly expenses and then our insurance costs and

Christmas and birthdays, there just isn't enough."

As I visited with this attractive, thirtysomething couple, I could see that they did not desire to build wealth for greed's sake. They really wanted to be able to give more to their church, and Jeff wanted to do less moonlighting and spend better time with their two children. Long-range, they were concerned about paying for the kids' college education. And someday, they wanted to retire in good enough shape so they wouldn't have to rely on Social Security and their children.

But despite these honorable goals, Jeff and MaryAnn seemed stuck on a paycheck-to-paycheck treadmill. Their consumer debt burden demanded inordinate chunks of each month's available cash, and the budgetary pressures didn't seem to want to go away. Because they were so preoccupied with present obligations, their desires for future financial accomplishments were only wishful thinking.

Jeff and MaryAnn's situation shows us that financial pressures are not just a problem for those of lower income. A Reader's Digest/Gallup Survey revealed that "36 percent of families with annual incomes of more than $25,000 frequently have trouble meeting their monthly bills," and that "65 percent of these relatively well-off Americans have had to change life-styles to cut expenses."[1]

PARKINSON'S SECOND LAW

Upon publication of his insightful book *The Law and the Profits* in 1960, C. Northcote Parkinson became famous in management circles for his now-classic Parkinson's Law: "Work expands to fill the time available." This perceptive author was pointing out that no matter how much time you're able to save in the workplace, your workload will always increase to fill the time you thought you had saved.

What many people do not remember is that within the same book, Parkinson made a second statement that in my opinion is even more prophetic than the first: "Expenditures rise to meet income."

Anyone who has ever managed a personal budget knows just how true this insight is. Have you, like thousands of others, ever promised yourself, "After my next raise, I'm going to get out of debt and save more"—only to see your personal expenses rise to equal or surpass the amount of the raise?

And have you, like thousands of others, promised yourself that if you can just get your debts paid off, you'll never go that deeply in debt again—only to see your debt balance grow to even higher heights than before?

If you have, you're not alone. No matter how good our intentions might be, Parkinson pointed out that "individual expenditure not only rises to meet income but tends to surpass it, and probably always will."[2]

This was Jeff and MaryAnn's dilemma. Despite their good intentions and above-average income, their haphazard spending patterns had conformed to Parkinson's Second Law and placed them in financial bondage. Now they felt immobilized—unable to chart a specific course of action to get out of debt and build for their future.

WHERE PROBLEMS COME FROM

Whether we're in big trouble or merely seeking to avoid trouble in the future, identifying some of the major problem sources is half the battle in our quest for financial freedom.

Remember Dr. Seuss's Grinch who stole Christmas? Picture a green, greedy monster like the Grinch, only call him "Crunch." He wants to steal your financial freedom away from you. Then picture him surrounded by a pack of green, greedy brothers—seven "Cash Crunches" all slavering for your money.

THE INFLATION/RECESSION CRUNCH

When this split-personality giant decides to rumble he can do some real damage.

Inflation (when too many dollars are available for too few goods) decreases the purchasing power of the dollar, thus requiring more dollars for the same goods. Its net effect is an actual decline in the wage earner's real disposable income, for salary increases can rarely keep pace with price increases when inflation is running loose.

Recession, on the other hand, has too few dollars available for too many goods. As a result, prices and interest rates may decline temporarily, but so will salary increases and available jobs as employers downsize to survive the slowdown in sales.

THE EMERGENCY CRUNCH

This rude, belligerent creature always shows up uninvited. He visits in forms both small and large. In his smaller visitations he is the surprise tax assessment due and payable last Tuesday, the unexpected guests who drop in for two weeks, the transmission job on the car, the porcelain dental crown. In Emergency's more obese forms, he is the lost job, the extensive medical tests, the damage done by tornado, earthquake, fire, or burglary. In chapter 9, we'll look at some strategies to help you be better prepared for this Cash Crunch.

M
A
N
T
A
L
K

THE "THING" CRUNCH

While we have little individual control over our national economy or emergencies, we *can* exercise some control over Thing and the next four Cash Crunches. They are all attitudes and misconceptions about money that we've allowed to infiltrate our thinking and distract us from sound financial management practices.

Thing is the product of an otherwise sound free-enterprise system. Over decades of unequaled prosperity, our society has taken on a Thing orientation which tends to emphasize the building of inventory over the building of character. Thing's advertisements bombard us right and left until our desires for the new car, new workout equipment, new computer, and new furniture become insatiable. And not only do we want to obtain these keys to happiness, we want to *get them now!*

THE "GET IT NOW" CRUNCH

This is the wart-nosed twin brother of Thing, born clinging to his brother's heel. He insists that since we want the Thing so badly, there's absolutely no reason why we should have to wait for it. Why plan or save for it when we can take the Thing home today and pay in easy installments for the next three decades? After all, we owe it to ourselves.

THE "KEEPING UP" CRUNCH

This critter often appears cross-eyed from constantly watching others from the corner of his eye. He's in close company with Thing and Get It Now. If Jones buys a new car, Keeping Up insists it's time we get one too. If Smith gets a promotion and travels to Europe on the extra salary, Keeping Up convinces us that we deserve a big vacation even if our finances barely allow a trip to McDonald's. This particular money monster can even pit husband against wife: If wife gets a new outfit, husband is then justified in buying a new CD system for his car.

THE "SAVE!" CRUNCH

How often in each day do we hear "Save 20 percent!" "Save $50 off regular price!" "Come on down and buy your new sofa now—and SAVE!!!"

Save? Think about it. Despite this Crunch's lucrative come-ons, there is no way one saves money when one spends it. He will only have fewer dollars in his pocket, or a higher balance on his charge account, than before. We do not save by spending, no matter how much the price has been reduced. Hundreds of families every year "save" themselves straight to bankruptcy court by grabbing more bargains than they can pay for.

THE "EASY CREDIT" CRUNCH

You'll find Easy Credit drooling over the shoulders of all six of his cronies. He's right there to help us keep on spending through tough economic times and emergencies; he's ever-ready, ever-faithful in helping us "make that bargain purchase possible" whenever the urge strikes to take home a Thing now or to Keep Up or Save!

When properly used, credit can be a worthwhile asset. But recent studies, which we'll look at a bit later, indicate that Easy Credit has bedeviled a lot of well-intentioned people.

A TIMELESS BATTLE

The seven Cash Crunches are not really new to our day and age, for most of the above tendencies have been in place since prehistoric man traded two flintstones for a Big Mac Raw. Proverbs, written approximately three thousand years ago, is filled with timeless advice about personal money management. A quick sampler:

On borrowing: "Just as the rich rule the poor, so the borrower is servant to the lender" (Proverbs 22:7, TLB).

On cosigning of notes: "Do not be among those who give pledges, among those who become sureties for debts. If you have nothing with which to pay, why should he take your bed from under you?" (Proverbs 22:26-27, NASB).

On the importance of planning and saving: "A prudent man foresees the difficulties ahead and prepares for them; the simpleton goes blindly on and suffers the consequences" (Proverbs 22:3, TLB). "The wise man saves for the future, but the foolish man spends whatever he gets" (Proverbs 21:20, TLB).

On making wealth your goal in life: "Do not weary yourself to gain wealth; cease from your consideration of it. When you set your eyes on it, it is gone. For wealth certainly makes itself wings, like an eagle that flies toward the heavens" (Proverbs 23:4-5, NASB).

While it is vanity to chase after wealth, the Bible does not deny that money is a necessity for survival, for sharing with others, and for enjoyment. Jesus Christ's parable of the talents, recorded in Matthew 25:14-30, presents a vivid picture of how God condemns financial slothfulness and encourages the prudent investment of our assets. So if common sense doesn't make the point strongly enough, we have the command direct from God to exercise wisdom in all money matters.

And have you ever stopped to think about how much money goes through your hands in a lifetime?

The average wage earner now in his twenties will earn and manage well over one million dollars. So for above-average earners like Jeff and MaryAnn, *more* money is really not the answer to their problems. Until they blend some discipline with some smart planning for the future, more money will only result in more taxes, spending, and debt. Expenditures rise to meet income. The answer to their need is not more money, but smarter management of what they do have.

THE DIFFERENCE BETWEEN SUCCESS AND FAILURE

I remember a young couple who talked with me following a financial planning seminar. Married just seven months, they had accumulated debts of more than $17,000 on several credit cards for furniture, clothing, and appliances. Interest rates for these purchases averaged more than 19 percent annually, obligating them to approximately $3200 per year in interest payments alone. With monthly take-home pay of $2200 and minimum monthly credit card payments totaling $1200, they were hard-pressed to pay their rent, purchase food, and provide for the other necessities of life. Savings and investment, of course, were out of the picture entirely.

On the other hand, I've had the privilege of meeting several individuals and couples with similar (and sometimes smaller) incomes, who had been able to build a small fortune in savings and investments while giving generously to charity and providing for both the necessities and the fun activities of life. The financial freedom they enjoyed enabled them to give even more to those in need, to live and travel debt-free, to enjoy golden years of financial dignity instead of financial poverty, and to focus more attention on the deeper, more important issues of life.

What makes the difference? Why is it that one couple lives in financial freedom while other couples of similar income and circumstances live just three weeks from bankruptcy?

In consulting with hundreds of men and women and studying profiles of dozens more, my colleagues and I found three "common denominators" of financial health among those who were financially successful:

1. *They each maintained specific, written, financial goals.*
2. *They each avoided debt financing on anything that does not appreciate in value.*
3. *They each invested a portion of every dollar for their future.*

Jeff and MaryAnn's lack of financial progress was a direct result of not following these three fundamentals.

First, while they had some dreams and ideas of what they would like to do "someday," they did not have a written list of specific financial goals. As a result, they were susceptible to the whims and temptations of the seven Cash Crunches.

Second, they always felt "too far in debt," despite all their good intentions not to overuse credit cards. Servicing these debts consumed dollars they could have been putting toward more constructive use.

Third, because of their haphazard spending patterns and resulting debt load, they had difficulty setting funds aside for future needs and goals. This meant that whenever one of those needs would come along, they had to pay for it from current cash flow or, more likely, by incurring further consumer debt.

YOU *CAN* SUCCEED WITH YOUR MONEY

If this couple's situation is similar to yours, you can take heart. Within a few short months Jeff and MaryAnn turned their situation around—and you can, too! It doesn't matter whether you're single or married, young or old; by putting the three common denominators of success to work, you can succeed with your personal finances and enjoy financial freedom.

Do those objectives sound worthwhile? In the days that follow we're going to turn these three common denominators into practical action points.

TAKING ACTION

☐ *Think back on your past earning/spending patterns. To what degree has Parkinson's Second Law ("Expenditures rise to meet income") been true in your life? Why?*

☐ *Review the biblical references to money mentioned in this chapter. In just two or three sentences, write a personal philosophy of money management to help guide your future attitudes and decisions.*

☐ *On a scale of 1 to 10, rank the degree of success you feel you've achieved in each of these three areas:*

___*I/we maintain specific, written, financial goals.*

___*I/we avoid debt financing on perishable or depreciating items.*

___*I/we invest a portion of every dollar for the future.*

M
A
N
T
A
L
K

Set specific, written financial goals

PLANNING FOR FINANCIAL FREEDOM

Clear definition of goals is the keynote of success.
EDISON MONTGOMERY

The ancient world's wisest and richest ruler was apparently a strong believer in goal planning. In Proverbs 22:3 Solomon wrote: "A prudent man foresees the difficulties ahead and prepares for them; the simpleton goes blindly on and suffers the consequences" (TLB).

Biblical advice is always timeless—and true to form. Solomon's words are just as sound today as when he wrote them three thousand years ago. How many people do you know who seem to grope through life hoping for an elusive ship to come in "someday"? Then, after several years—sometimes decades—they look at their net worth and realize how little they have to show for all their labor. "Where does it all go?" they ask, shaking their heads helplessly.

Ask these people what their financial goals are and they usually reply, "To have more money," or, "To pay some bills." But ask them *how much* more money they're talking about or *when* they would like to have their bills paid, and they have difficulty being specific.

Jeff and MaryAnn were like that. They had never sat down together to organize a list of specific goals that would help them prioritize all their spending opportunities. As a result, their spending had been haphazard and subject to the frequent lures of instant gratification.

In our studies of clients and others who were financially successful, my colleagues and I discovered that almost without exception those who had achieved financial freedom were deliberate goal planners. Just as you and I couldn't fathom building a house without a set of blueprints, these successful people wouldn't consider building their "financial house" without a set of prioritized plans to guide them. Their financial goals help them sort through all the demands for their money and provide a blueprint to guide them in the best stewardship of their resources.

Goal planning can help you in the same way. With your own plan before you, you can avoid Jeff and MaryAnn's predicament of haphazard spending, too little savings, and too much debt. You'll begin to see financial progress, which up till now may not have seemed possible. But to be effective, your goals should be specific, measurable, achievable, and motivational. And they should be *in writing*.

MAKE YOUR GOALS SPECIFIC AND MEASURABLE

In our interviews with financial planning clients, we always asked about retirement goals. A common answer went like this: "I'd like to retire someday, with lots of money, and have lots of fun."

Such a goal statement was of little help because it was neither specific nor measurable. Unless we knew what our clients meant by "someday" and what they considered to be "lots of money," no strategies could be formulated or investment vehicles selected. These clients were like the proverbial archer who shoots his arrows into the air, then searches for each arrow and paints targets around them wherever they land. Without specific and measurable goals to guide their "aim," these clients will someday find themselves near retirement, wondering how they'll ever make it through the last twenty to thirty years of life.

In working with clients of all ages, my colleagues and I were able to help them be more specific in their goal planning. Once we knew that they would like to retire in twenty-four years with a paid-for home and a monthly income equal to $3500 in today's dollars, we could formulate a series of integrated financial strategies and select proper investment choices to help them achieve their goals.

Shorter-term goal setting can and should be just as specific. Instead of stating that you "want to have some money for a good vacation someday," decide specifically *when* you want to take the vacation, *how much money* you'll need to "do it right," and *where the funds will come from* between now and then. If you determine that you want to start the vacation in ten months and that you'll need $3000 for the trip, you can then examine your liquid assets and your anticipated income sources to formulate a plan for having the money on hand when vacation begins.

Being specific and measurable in your goal setting helps you know that you're planning for adequate future provision, and that you're not overplanning for more than you'll actually need. Even more important, specific and measurable goals let you know when you've arrived! That's the time to congratulate yourself and celebrate!

MAKE YOUR GOALS ACHIEVABLE AND MOTIVATIONAL

Setting unreachable targets can quickly de-motivate even the most positive-minded goal-setter. A married couple with a projected pension of $300 a month and just $2500 in the bank is not realistic in wanting to retire two years from now with a monthly income of $3500. Neither is the individual who wants to take a $3000 vacation in ten months if his cash flow allows him to set aside only $50 per month between now and then. Both of these parties will soon be disillusioned when they discover how unachievable their desires are.

It's okay to select targets that require some discipline and determination, but for the sake of your morale and self-confidence you will want to keep the goals reachable. Don't set goals that would require a surprise inheritance from your long-lost great aunt or a winning number in the Publishers Clearinghouse Sweepstakes. Your goals will be achievable if you can realistically foresee how various sources of necessary funds will come together to make your objectives happen on time.

You'll find that the most effective goals are also motivational—they are designed to help you accomplish the desires of your heart. Therefore, I recommend that you make your goals personally significant. Select goals that will bring honor to God, togetherness and security to your family, and personal joy to you. That way, if you're ever tempted to waste time or money along the way, you can remind yourself how important your personal goals are and steer clear of superficial expenditures.

PUT YOUR GOALS IN WRITING

One secret we noticed in our study of financially independent people is that they always plan their goals with pen in hand.

Written goals help you stay organized and focused. Your list becomes a sort of contract with yourself that keeps your personal priorities near the front of your mind and, as a result, prompts you to take disciplined, steady action toward their fulfillment. Steve Sitkowski, the successful young president of a large financial planning firm in Newport Beach, California, recommends writing your goals on the back of your business card and keeping the card in your wallet. Sitkowski says he reviews his personal list of goals almost every morning and asks himself, "What will I do *today* to help make these happen?" That list prompts him to schedule a specific block of time or make a special effort each day toward the achievement of his financial objectives.

I have found Sitkowski's method effective, with a few personal variations. Kathy and I plan our goals by the year, then break them down into quarterly goals. By abbreviating each goal with a few key words, I can write one quarter's list on the back of a business card. It includes not only Kathy's and my financial goals, but several spiritual, relational, and vocational goals as well.

GET READY TO DREAM

Remember the Achievement Progression? As we worked through it in chapter 3, we saw that "a goal is a dream with a deadline."

I like that definition. It puts the whole process in a nutshell for us. Successful goal planning is the art of identifying your dreams, putting them on paper, prioritizing them, and determining when and how you'd like to accomplish each one.

To help you identify those dreams, let me suggest that before you begin goal planning you read through the next two chapters. These discussions will trigger several ideas for you to consider as priorities in your own financial situation.

Then schedule a quiet, uninterrupted block of time for your personal goal planning. If you're married, you'll definitely want to include your wife in the process so you can work together as partners toward mutual objectives.

Find a place and time when your minds will be free to fly with ideas. Kathy and I have found that we enjoy goal planning in a restaurant or coffee shop. Three or four times a year we devote a leisurely breakfast to goal planning, and with pen and pad nearby we share dreams and ideas with each other. Sometimes we ask tough questions to help each other determine whether a particular idea is merely a whim or of true significance. We've learned to seek each other's feedback in determining whether a desire is in harmony with God's will for our lives. It's always a meaningful (sometimes revealing) time of communication, and two hours later we usually have a written set of mutual and individual goals on which we pledge to support each other.

Before you look into your future to dream of what you would like to accomplish, let me suggest that you both spend some time in prayer, asking God to guide you in his perfect will. We are told in Psalm 127:1 that "unless the Lord builds the house, its

MANTALK

builders labor in vain" (TLB). And Proverbs 16:3 instructs, "Commit to the Lord whatever you do, and your plans will succeed" (NIV). God's Word makes it clear that he is vitally interested in how we handle our finances, and he promises that "if any of you lacks wisdom, he should ask God, who gives generously to all without finding fault, and it will be given to him" (James 1:5, NIV).

After a time of prayer, you're ready to begin. You might find it helpful to ask yourselves questions such as the following:

IMMEDIATE CONCERNS (WITHIN THE NEXT 2 MONTHS)

- In what areas, if any, do we feel financially insecure at this time in our lives? Why?
  Consider:
  ___ Monthly cash flow
  ___ Liquid reserve for emergencies
  ___ Debt load
  ___ Insurance coverage for:
     ___ Death of a breadwinner
     ___ Long-term disability of a breadwinner
       ___ Major medical expense
       ___ Major damage to home and furnishings
       ___ Auto accidents and liabilities
       ___ Other liabilities

- What specific steps should we take to help feel more secure in our weak areas?
  Examples:
  ___ Go through our records and budget to determine how to spend $___ less per month and put those dollars into savings.

___Meet with at least two insurance brokers to check our insurance coverages for death, disability, homeowners, auto, and liability.

- By what date will we implement each of the above steps?

SHORT-TERM (WITHIN THE NEXT 2-12 MONTHS)

- What do you think our financial goals should be for the next two to twelve months?
  Consider:
  ___Charitable giving
  ___Emergency reserve
  ___Debt load
  ___Any goals from the "Immediate Concerns" list that still need work

- What specific steps should we begin taking *now* to accomplish our "Short-Term" goals within the next twelve months?
  Examples:
  ___Begin adding $___ to each month's donation to our church.
  ___Set up an automatic monthly transfer of $___ from our checking account to XYZ mutual fund
  ___Hold off on further charges to credit cards and add $___ per month to our payment

- By what date should we implement each step?

MEDIUM-TERM (WITHIN THE NEXT 1-3 YEARS)

- What should we try to accomplish financially within the next one to three years?
  Consider:
  ___College fund for children

___ Continuing education

___ New car(s)

___ Individual Retirement Accounts

___ Vacation fund

___ Goals from our "Short-Term" list that still need work

- What specific steps should we begin taking *now* to help us meet those goals?
  Examples:

  ___ Designate ___percent of our automatic transfer to mutual fund for IRA contributions

  ___ Begin setting aside ___percent of bonuses and miscellaneous earnings toward future car purchase

  ___ Set aside $___ per month for vacation and add from free-lance earnings

- By what date should we implement each step we've decided upon?

LONG-TERM (BEYOND 3 YEARS)

- What will financial freedom mean to us ten years from now? What will it mean to us when we retire?

- What should be our financial goals for three to ten years from now?
  Consider:

  ___ New home

  ___ Other investments

  ___ Own business

  ___ Children's or our own education

  ___ Leave of absence for volunteer service

  ___ Review and update of insurance program

  ___ Any goals from "Medium-Term" that still need work

- At what age would we like to retire? What would we like to do then for fun? For service to others? For continued personal growth?

- In today's dollars, what amount of monthly income would we need then to enjoy that life-style?

- What strategies do we need to begin implementing *now* so we will not have to depend on our children in our retirement years?

PRIORITIZE

After your initial thoughts and discussions, you may feel overwhelmed as you review several pages of scrawled handwriting and wonder how you'll ever have the time and money to accomplish everything you've listed. If you do, that's great! You're normal! Now it's time to sharpen your focus a bit.

Prayerfully go through your list and rank your goals, 1 through 10, in the order of importance to you. Then take the first five and write each one in the form of an optimistic goal statement:

I/we will *(goal to be accomplished)* by *(deadline)*. In order to assure this goal, I/we will *(specific action to be taken)* by *(date action is to begin)*.

As an example, let's say one of your top five goals is to fund your Individual Retirement Account with $2000 for the current tax year. It's now May, and since the law gives you until April 15 of the next calendar year to complete your contribution, you have twelve months in which to accumulate the $2000. Your written goal might read like this:

I/we will *have $2000 in my IRA by April 15.* In order to assure this goal, I/we will *contribute $166.67 per* *month by automatic deduction from our checking account* beginning *the fifteenth of this month.*

Try to be as specific with your other goals as well, for this list will guide and motivate you during the coming weeks and months. Using key words and abbreviations, summarize the list on a small card and keep it in your wallet. You may also want to make extra copies to place in your checkbook, on your desk, on your bathroom mirror. Daily, review each of your five goals and ask yourself:

"What will I do *today* to help make these happen?"

Then take appropriate action.

If you're like me, you'll enjoy the actual process of "checking off" each goal as you achieve it. It's an opportunity to praise the Lord for his provision and to celebrate another step toward financial freedom. Success breeds success, so you'll be motivated to keep at it.

But you won't want to bask too long in the thrill of victory. Once you accomplish a goal, add another one from your Top Ten list—or a fresh new goal that has come to mind. Successful people constantly update and revise their goals to be sure that the most important priorities are addressed as needed.

In chapter 8, we'll look at one area that should be a big part of everyone's goal planning: getting and keeping your debts under control.

TAKING ACTION

☐ *Schedule a two-hour time within the next week for uninterrupted goal planning. If you are married or engaged, make it a time for mutual sharing and dreaming.*

☐ *Follow the guidelines in this chapter to write
goal statements for your five most important
financial objectives.*

☐ *Make copies of your five goals on small cards.
Place one in your wallet(s) and one in your
checkbook.*

M

A

N

T

A

L

K

> **Avoid debt financing on anything that does not appreciate in value.**

ESCAPING THE DEBT TRAP

Whatever you have, spend less.
SAMUEL JOHNSON

"What would you do if you had all the money in the world?" Harold asked Ted.

"I'd apply it to my debts, as far as it would go," Ted replied.

Have you ever felt like Ted? Like your debts are mounting faster than your ability to pay them? Like you could do so many positive things if only you could get out of debt"?

Credit can be a tremendous asset to individuals and families who respect it for what it is: a tool to help them acquire appreciating assets such as a home, investment real estate, a promising business, or other select assets. In business a strong line of credit is essential for capital investment as well as a buffer against the inevitable ups and downs of cash flow.

The reality of our society is that good credit is necessary for much of the routine buying of life. Lenders want to see a positive credit history before they loan us money for our new home, automobile, college education, or business venture. And a valid credit card is almost mandatory for renting a car or writing a check.

But like most good things in life, credit is meant to be used wisely and not abused. Where many of us get into some trouble is in the use of *consumer credit:* those charge cards, credit cards, loans-by-mail, and even home equity loans that are used for perishable or depreciating items. Because consumer credit is so accessible, the average American installment debt grew from $239 in 1960 to well over $2700 before the end of the 1980s.[1] One recent report found that "a small but beleaguered minority are enslaved to mountainous consumer-debt burdens that exceed *half their annual incomes*" (emphasis added).[2]

THE PITCH

We live in a time when credit card companies virtually beg us to sign up for high credit limits and immediate cash advances of thousands of dollars. Almost every week, my mail contains a letter from the president of a bank in Anywhere, USA, which begins something like this:

> *Dear Mr. and Mrs. Benson:*
>
> *Because you are such pillars of your community and have such an outstanding credit history, we are extending to you an invitation to own our beautiful platinum credit card. . . .*

The letter goes on to extol the incredible peace of mind we will have once that platinum card is in our possession. Why, for a low annual fee of just $75 (which, for our convenience, we can charge to our new card) this nice bank president will send us a check for our first $5000 to tide us over until our personally engraved platinum card arrives. (We can have more money if we want it by simply requesting a higher amount on the handy "Make Your Dreams Come True" reservation form.)

The letter urges us to imagine the prestige we will feel when we whip that card out for a new wardrobe, a dream vacation, a new CD-stereo system, or big-screen TV . . . and more cash advances whenever we want, at thousands of convenient locations around the world.

BUT WAIT! THERE'S MORE!

That's right, there are still more benefits to carrying our very own platinum credit card from the Anywhere Bank. Every time we charge a purchase to our card we accrue "points" toward a beautiful gift of our choice. Earn enough points and we'll qualify for an executive datebook bound in rich Corinthian plastic. Additional points qualify us for a luxurious pen and pencil set, a seven-speed blender, or a cordless facial hair remover.

By now we're supposed to be so excited about all the neat things we can do with our very own platinum credit card that we'll totally ignore the hidden message of the mailing. What the nice bank president doesn't put in his letter (but *does* put in tiny print on the back of the handy "Make Your Dreams Come True" reservation form) is that he expects us to pay him back all this money he's giving us. And not only does he expect to be paid back, he's going to charge a near-usurious rate of nondeductible interest and try to get us to stretch out our payments until the day the Sun City Lawn Bowlers win the Super Bowl. These extended payments will earn him additional interest, enabling him to buy his daughter Muffy a new Mercedes for her sixteenth birthday.

Frankly, I would rather save all that interest so I can get my own new Mercedes or my own cordless facial hair remover. But do you see how easy it is to be lured by all the offers from the Credit-Card-of-the-Month Club? A decade ago, banks approved between 30 and 50 percent of all credit-card applications. Within just a few years, the acceptance rate was 40 to 60 percent. The average American adult now owns seven or eight cards,[3] and banks, department stores, and financial institutions mount aggressive advertising campaigns to convince unwary consumers that they can live now in the manner to which they hope to become accustomed.

ONE COUPLE'S STORY

One couple, Michael and Cynthia, never asked for their first credit cards. When they were both thirty years old, offers for four cards showed up in their mailbox.

Michael and Cynthia were well-educated and together they brought home a good income. "We used credit cards for whatever caught our fancy," Cynthia recalls. They drew frequent cash advances and made only minimum payments. Whenever they reached the credit limit on one card, they started spending on another.

Within five years this couple owed more than $32,000 on sixty-three credit cards. With their payments running at least six weeks late, all those nice bank presidents sent more letters—only now the letters had a nasty tone and demanded payment.

Michael and Cynthia report that the stress of being so far in debt nearly tore them apart.[4]

This couple's consumer debt burden was far above the national average, but their story is indicative of the way Americans slip into the trap of "If the shoe fits, charge it." According to the Federal Reserve, we carry more than $600 billion in consumer debt (which does not include home mortgages). This is double the level of the early '80s. It is interesting that personal bankruptcies also doubled during the last decade.[5]

Typically, people do not acquire credit cards with the intention of running them up into the stratosphere. The usual rationale for the first card or two or three is that "it's good to have for emergencies" or for identification when writing personal checks. But then the emergency vacation and the emergency VCR and the emergency dinner out always seem to strike when cash is short—besides, we'll pay off the full amount when the statement comes, right?

But when that moment of truth comes, other pressing needs have arrived. So we'll just send in the minimum payment. Then, during the next month, other emergencies become just too good to pass up. And so it goes: Buy now, pay forever.

THE WAGES OF MISUSED CREDIT

Our "instant gratification" syndrome, combined with too-easy credit, robs many of us of the ability and incentive to plan, save, and build for our futures. This is what had happened to Michael and Cynthia and to Jeff and MaryAnn whom we met earlier. Their cash flow was so consumed paying for perished or depreciating items that they were unable to build their own emergency reserve, save for planned expenditures, invest for their retirement years, or give to their church or favorite charity. They were in financial bondage.

In his play *A Doll's House,* Henrik Ibsen wrote, "There can be no freedom or beauty about a home life that depends on borrowing or debt." Indeed, as my colleagues and I consulted with clients from moderate to high income levels, we found that ensnarement in consumer debt is one of the primary reasons people fail to attain financial freedom. Successful people keep consumer credit under control, borrowing with discretion and only for appreciating assets.

HOW TO RECOGNIZE A DEBT PROBLEM

Nice bank presidents suddenly lose their sanguine spirit when borrowers fail to make minimum payments on schedule. Therefore, financial experts generally agree that one's consumer debts (debts other than home mortgages) should not exceed 15 to 20 percent of after-tax income. That should be considered an absolute maximum limit. If your total consumer debt load exceeds 20 percent of annual take-home pay, you're in way over your head.

In addition to the above limits, there are several other key indicators to alert you that your consumer debt situation is getting out of line:

___You consistently pay only the minimum amount due each month on your installment or credit card expenses.

___You tend to add more expenses to an account than you can pay off at the end of the same month.

___You have an inner "lack of peace" about your debt situation.

___You find you must charge perishable or depreciating items that you formerly purchased with cash.

___You've received some late-payment penalties or some letters or phone calls about late payments.

___You're unable to consistently put at least 5 percent of your after-tax income toward savings and investment.

The more savvy financial consultants will tell you that it's best to carry *no* consumer debts. Consumer items by definition rarely appreciate in value, so they cannot be excused as "investments." And since 1990, when tax deductions were phased out for consumer-loan interest, we can no longer use the rationale that Uncle Sam helps defray our interest expense.

It's actually a smart investment these days to pay consumer debts in full—and keep them current. Assuming the average interest rate on your installment loans and credit cards is 20 percent, when you pay your bill in full you've received a virtual *20 percent earning* on investment by eliminating that interest obligation from your cash flow. Therefore, avoiding finance charges is the surest investment you can possibly make—a guaranteed return of 20 percent!

IF YOU'RE IN TOO DEEP . . .

If you're dog-paddling in debt and the indicators tell you you're overextended, don't allow masculine pride, embarrassment, or fear of losing your credit rating keep you from seeking help. Your personal reputation and credit record are too important for you *not* to take corrective action.

1. *Admit to yourself that things are out of hand.* Go through all your records and make a list of all your

creditors, including their addresses, phone numbers, the amount you owe, the rate of interest, and the minimum monthly payment. As you look back through your records, try to spot unwise purchases and draw some conclusions about your spending patterns.

2. *Hold a family financial council on the budget.* Until your children reach the teen years, this council would probably include just you and your wife. But as children become older and carry more responsibility, make finances a family affair. Be honest about the problem, and present it as an opportunity to work together as a team in solving it. Instead of presenting an autocratic decree for cutting back, ask each family member to suggest ways to reduce spending and come up with extra funds to apply to debt reduction.

3. *Commit to each other that you will incur no further consumer debt.* Lock the credit cards in a safety deposit box or destroy them if necessary. From this day forward, operate on a cash, pay-as-you-go basis. One couple actually froze their credit cards in a water-filled milk carton, knowing that having to thaw out their cards before a purchase would force them to pause and think whether they really "needed" to put the desired item on credit.

4. If you feel you cannot keep up with your minimum monthly payments, *seek help from a nonprofit credit counseling agency such as the National Foundation for Consumer Credit.* A good credit counselor will have been in the business at least five years and will charge you nothing or a minimal fee. He or she will take your cards away and put you on an aggres-

sive payback schedule, but the strict discipline may be just what you need to escape the debt trap and get your finances back in order.

5. *Set up a system for eliminating your consumer debts.* An excellent do-it-yourself system for personal debt elimination is DEBTFREE, available for $14.95 from Financial Services Network. The kit includes complete instructions and easy-to-use charts to help you get organized, systematically reduce and eliminate your debt load, and build your personal savings. Send check or money order for $14.95 to Financial Services Network, 600 Grant Street, Suite 506, Denver, CO 80203. (Colorado residents add 6.5 percent sales tax.)

STRATEGIES TO KEEP CREDIT IN LINE

If you've managed to keep your own consumer debt situation under control, you are to be commended for your diligence. You've avoided one of the most lethal financial traps in existence today, and you have greater freedom to pursue the savings and investment objectives we'll be discussing in the next chapter. Following are some important strategies to help you maintain a healthy debt profile:

1. *If you do have an accumulated balance on a charge card or credit card, pay it down to zero.* The sooner you do so, the sooner you can apply those principal and interest payments to more important things in life. When writing your monthly check to the lender, take the minimum monthly payment required, add anything you may have charged during the last month, then add an additional $25, $50, or more. Repeat this process every month until your past obligations are down to zero.

2. *Determine the maximum you will charge to your credit card in a given month.* With your spouse, agree on a monthly dollar limit you will not go beyond, no matter what temptations come your way. It should be a sum you feel you can comfortably pay *in full* upon arrival of the monthly statement, without sacrificing other areas of your budget.

3. *Ask yourself some tough questions.* The fact that you've determined a maximum monthly limit for credit-card spending does not obligate you to spend up to that limit every month. So when the urge strikes, ask yourself some tough questions to see if the purchase is really necessary. Start with "Why do I want this? Is it a whim that I'll regret in a week?" Then ask yourself, "Will I want this item as badly in thirty days when the bill comes?" Some smart couples actually make themselves walk out of a store to discuss, pray, and "sleep on" a major purchase before committing themselves (good advice, even when intending to pay with cash). "It's amazing," one husband told me, "how much that item back in the store decreases in importance after a night's sleep."

4. *Pay each credit card purchase in full upon arrival of the statement.* Without exception, do not allow payment of a charge to be delayed into a future month. A practical way to accomplish this objective is to actually deduct a credit card purchase from your checking account ledger on the same day you incur the obligation. Make a clear note to yourself regarding the purchase, *circle it*, then deduct the amount of the purchase from your checking account total. When the credit card statement arrives, the total of your circled items should be the same as the

M

A

N

T

A

L

K

total of credit-card charges for the month. Since the funds have already been deducted from your checking account ledger, you're able to write a check to the credit card company paying your new charges in full.

5. *Avoid future debt burdens and finance charges by saving in advance for major purchases.* Exercising discipline in debt management enables you to be much more aggressive in your savings program. And by saving in advance for future needs, you can help prevent future debt obligations and costly finance charges. So if you haven't already done so, now's the time to begin setting funds aside for that future vacation, automobile, refrigerator, wardrobe, you-name-it. All of these items should be paid in full upon purchase.*

By saving in advance for major needs, you will not only avoid debt-servicing obligations in the future, but you will also be earning interest instead of *paying* interest.

Prudent debt management is worth the effort! If you can keep your consumer spending and debt burden under control you'll feel a greater sense of security, control, and peace of mind. You'll have extra funds to use in more constructive ways, like saving for future *interest-free* purchases, or a college education for your children, or your own business start-up. And most importantly, you'll be able to be financially independent when retirement time comes, free from dependence on your children or charity.

*For realistic reasons, the only exception to the above might be the automobile. Few items depreciate as rapidly, but new car prices often make financing a necessity. You can minimize the fiscal impact of this purchase by accumulating a substantial down payment in advance and shopping around for the best financing available. Consumer experts say you'll find the best value by purchasing a well-maintained car that's two to three years old, for the heavy depreciation will have reduced its price remarkably with relatively little wear and tear on the car.

Our next discussion will help you achieve those dreams.

TAKING ACTION

☐ *Total all your personal debts other than the first mortgage on your house. Then divide the total by your annual take-home pay to determine the percentage of after-tax income your debts represent.*

☐ *What specific spending tendencies has this chapter shed light upon that you would like to change?*

☐ *With your spouse, review the recommendations of this chapter and agree on at least three specific strategies you will implement immediately to get and keep consumer debt under control.*

M

A

N

T

A

L

K

**Invest a
portion of
every dollar for
your future.**

9

BUILDING
FINANCIAL
FREEDOM

*The wise man saves for the future,
but the foolish man spends whatever he gets.*
SOLOMON (Proverbs 21:20, TLB)

Your wife's doctor orders a hospital stay complete with tests, surgery and $25-per-tissue Kleenex. Your wife is fine now, but when all the paper work has settled, you're stuck with several thousand dollars in deductibles and copayments.

The car you had hoped to keep alive for three more years has just gasped, clutched its chest, and died. Suddenly you're looking at new cars, wondering how you're going to handle the exorbitant monthly payments.

The time to launch your own business has never looked better. The market is ready for your product or service. But getting a good start requires money, and lenders are asking you what *you're* willing to invest from your own pocket.

The boss has a somber look. "Close the door," he says as you enter his office. "I'm deeply sorry, but as you know we're going through a tough time here at Wally's Widget World. We have to let you go."

You're hoping to retire in five years. But as you add up what you're likely to receive from Social Security and your company pension, the future doesn't look so golden after all.

Emergencies. Opportunities. Loss of income. At some point in our lives, most of us will encounter scenarios like the ones above. We've been around the block enough times to know that current income doesn't always meet current expenses. Life's surprises just do not time themselves to fit neatly within our monthly cash flow.

And then there are future financial events that should come as no surprise, like the kids' college education. Or retirement—when a gold watch suddenly replaces a steady paycheck. The uncertainties of life, combined with future certainties, underscore the importance of building an accessible financial reserve.

And therein lies our third common denominator of financial success. *Of every dollar you earn, invest a portion for your future.* Solomon phrased it well: "The wise man saves for the future, but the foolish man spends whatever he gets" (Proverbs 21:20, TLB).

WHY SAVE?

Americans have not been the most prudent of savers. During the past decade we saved as little as 3.2 percent of our disposable income and as much as 5 percent. When you compare these averages with those of the Japanese, who typically save between 15 and 20 percent, it's easy to see that setting aside a portion of our earnings for the future has not been a priority in U. S. households.

But many economists predict that our motives for saving might grow stronger during the next decade, when the Baby Boomers—the 76 million Americans born between 1946 and 1964—reach middle age. As one economist said recently:

> *They [the Baby Boomers] already own every item on the planet, so buying demand is running out of steam. And when they see their parents developing financial and health problems, it's going to scare the dickens out of them.*[1]

Yet, despite a stronger savings motive, many men and women continue to find excuses to put off the most important step in achieving financial freedom.

"I'll start saving when I get my next raise."
"When I get my debts paid off."
"After the first of the year, when Christmas is over."
"We've got some stuff we've been wanting to get."
"We just don't have anything left to save!"
"Someday, when my ship comes in."

On the surface, all of these reasons might sound legitimate. But what usually happens while we're waiting for the "right" time to begin saving money? If Parkinson's Second Law holds true and expenditures rise to meet income, by the time our next raise comes along or our debts are paid off, we'll have found other necessities on which to spend available dollars.

In the short run, procrastination can only lead to further debt and difficulty when we're required to face emergencies and other expenses with little or no accessible reserves.

In the long run, procrastination usually compounds into near-destitution during what should be the best years of our lives. According to Social Security Administration statistics, only a small number of our citizens are financially independent upon reaching age 65. The vast majority find that their Social Security benefits, pensions (if available), and personal savings are not enough to cover the expenses of their senior years. They then must continue working at whatever employment they can find or get help from their children or charity.[2]

Unfortunately, this is the likely result for the individual or couple who do not make a conscientious effort to invest a portion of their earnings for the future. One recent report forecasts the situation this way:

> *Someone who plans to retire in 30 years at age 65, and who would like a yearly income equivalent to $45,000 in today's dollars for another 25 years or so, may need an annual income of $146,000 by his retirement in 2019, rising to $389,000 by the time he's 90 because of the sandpapering effect of inflation. . . . Even if Social Security and a pension provide 60 percent of his retirement income, he would need a nest egg of some $1.1 million to close the gap.[3]*

OTHER TIMES MONEY WILL BE NEEDED

And let's be realistic: Retirement isn't the only time of life when a strong financial reserve is necessary. Every one of us can look forward to one or more of the following:

Down payment on a first house
Vacations
Down payments on new cars
Replenishment of wardrobes
Children's college expenses
Children's weddings
Medical and dental expenses
Leaves of absence
Care for ill or elderly parents
Annual, semiannual, or quarterly insurance premiums
Home maintenance and repairs
Car maintenance and repairs
Household appliance repair or replacement
Furniture or decor upgrades
A friend or ministry in need of financial help
Christmas, birthdays, anniversaries
Business opportunities
Business losses
Investment opportunities
Loss of income due to layoff or disability.

You may be experiencing some of these circumstances right now. As long as you have a pulse, you can *count on* some of them visiting you in the future. Would you like to be able to deal with these situations without having to go into debt?

Your chances of doing so will be dramatically enhanced if you begin now to invest a portion of every dollar you earn for your future.

I know, I know. Someone out there is thinking, *But you don't know my situation! With my budget, there just isn't anything left to save!*

This is one of the most common frustrations of those who are unsuccessful in building financial freedom. And let's face it—it *is* tough out there! Costs don't go down; they go up. Wages rarely keep pace. How is it possible to put money in savings when the demand always seems to outstrip the supply?

SUCCESSFUL SAVINGS: THE REAL SECRET

The foundational secret to savings success is amazingly simple. It is found in George S. Clason's classic book *The Richest Man in Babylon*. The author opens the story with a description of his title character:

> *In old Babylon there once lived a certain very rich man named Arkad. Far and wide he was famed for his wealth. Also was he famed for his liberality. He was generous in his charities. He was generous with his family. He was liberal in his own expenses. But nevertheless each year his wealth increased more rapidly than he spent it.*

How had Arkad come across his great wealth? Had his Aunt Grizelda handed it down to him? Had he won the state Lotto jackpot?

His friends had similar questions. They had gone to the same schools as Arkad and worked just as hard. Yet they were barely keeping their heads above the financial waters. One day they asked him, "Why, then, should a fickle fate single you out to enjoy all the good things of life and ignore us who are equally deserving?"

Arkad was happy to share his secret with them. He replied that he had discovered the foundational secret to financial success when he realized one simple truth: "A part of all I earn is mine to keep."

At first his friends laughed, for they had always thought that all they earned was theirs to keep. But quickly they realized that all their money went to other people: tax collectors, bakers, sandlemakers, wine makers—leaving nothing for themselves.

Arkad, on the other hand, had decided early in his career to set aside one-tenth of his earnings for future needs and opportunities. At first it wasn't easy. But after several months it became a habit and he didn't even miss the money that he saved. Through a series of experiences he learned how to make good investments, and his wealth grew. All the while, he was generous to those in need around him.[4]

In one simple sentence, the author of this story has identified the foundational secret to successful savings: *"A part of all I earn is mine to keep."* You will note that Arkad did not hoard his finances; nor did he hedge on his taxes or compromise his business relationships. Rather, he shared generously with those in need and conducted business with utmost integrity. And "each year his wealth increased more rapidly than he spent it." Because of his savings habit and the investments he made with those reserves, Arkad was able to increase his giving, offer employment to citizens of his community, and provide for the future needs and dreams of his family.

FROM AFTERTHOUGHT TO PRIORITY

Today, because of a high level of personal spending, most individuals and couples regard personal savings as an afterthought. They follow the pattern of Arkad's friends, paying out first for all their monthly expenses and then seeing if there is anything left for savings.

But as Arkad found, the key to success is to reverse the usual procedure. Instead of forking out all your funds to expenses and ending up with only lint in your pockets, "pay yourself first" by sending a specific percentage of your after-tax income to savings *before you pay any other bills.*

This commitment is the best guarantee that you'll be setting something aside every month, regardless of other expenses. If you are still eliminating some heavy debts, you might start saving as little as 2 or 3 percent of your take-home pay. Then commit to increasing your savings percentage by 2 points each year until you are setting aside a minimum of 10 percent of your net income every month.

HOW TO MAKE IT HAPPEN

If you haven't been paying yourself first before now, this practice may take some adjustment. The first month or two might be tough. But don't give up! Like young Arkad, you will discover that your budget will soon mold itself around your new priorities, and within six months you won't even miss the dollars that are going to savings.

One of the best ways to make certain you pay yourself first is to set up an automatic draft from your personal checking account to a money market fund. (Several funds offer such programs; you can find their toll-free numbers in the popular personal finance magazines.)

I remember how Gary and Nicole turned their finances around using the "pay yourself first" strategy. They had been unable to save much during the first twelve years of their marriage. After discussing their monthly expenses, they agreed to designate 10 percent of their after-tax income to savings.

At first, they admitted, adjusting to their new cash flow required some self-discipline. But after just three months they realized they no longer missed the $200 per month that was automatically going to savings. After one year they saw that their money market fund balance totalled $2400, plus reinvested earnings—more than they had been able to accumulate in the previous twelve years! This motivated them to keep going—and to gradually increase the amount they were designating to savings.

THE 10-10-80 PLAN

With the new priority they were giving to personal savings, Gary and Nicole's budget could be summarized like this:

OF NET (AFTER-TAX) INCOME:
10 percent Giving
10 percent Long-term Savings and Investment
80 percent Living Expenses (includes short-term
savings)

This 10-10-80 budget plan (and variations thereof) is frequently recommended by financial consultants. If you feel there is room for improvement in your personal finances, you may want to give it serious consideration as one of your financial goals for the coming year. Here is how it worked for Gary and Nicole.

10 PERCENT GIVING

A generous spirit is essential to financial freedom. I believe giving should be everyone's top priority, both as an investment in society and as an act of gratitude for the blessings we receive. For dedicated Christians like Gary and Nicole, giving takes on even greater significance: It is an indication of the priority we give God in our lives. Gary and Nicole gave a regular tithe of their income to the ministry of their church, and placed this first in their list of monthly expenditures. And they considered the tithe their *minimum* amount for giving; often they would spot other opportunities to give to other ministries or to someone in need. For these situations they would pull money from their living expenses allotment or short-term savings.

10 PERCENT LONG-TERM SAVINGS AND INVESTMENT

The automatic monthly draft from Gary and Nicole's checking account helped assure that 10 percent of their take-home pay went to long-term savings. They agreed that except for a dire emergency they would not touch this growing reserve. To benefit from compounding, they authorized the fund to automatically reinvest all dividend earnings.

Gary and Nicole's long-range priorities for these dollars were as follows:

1. *Emergency Reserve.* The first long-range goal they wanted to accomplish was setting aside three months' living expenses in an emergency reserve. This was their "peace of mind" fund for an extreme emergency such as a job layoff or a major household repair or medical expense. Once they accumulated three months' living expenses they moved the emergency reserve to another money market fund to separate it from their other long-range savings. If they ever needed to use part of the reserve, Gary and Nicole considered it a priority to replenish what they used as quickly as possible.

2. *Individual Retirement Accounts.* Even though Gary had a pension plan at his company, they agreed that it would be prudent not to plan on the pension and Social Security providing for all of their golden-year

needs. So Individual Retirement Accounts were next on their list of long-range savings objectives. They set up an account for each of them and began using a major portion of their long-range savings dollars to make the maximum allowable contributions to their IRAs each year.

3. *Other Investments.* As time passed and Gary and Nicole received pay increases, they were able to gradually increase the amount they were designating to long-term savings and investment. They continued to fund their IRAs each year, and with the ongoing advice of financial consultants they used additional savings dollars to diversify among other investments. From these investments they planned to help provide for their children's college education, start a small decorating business for Nicole, and enjoy some travel and volunteer opportunities later in life.

80 PERCENT LIVING EXPENSES

Of course, the key to the 10-10-80 Plan is learning to live on 80 percent of your net income. If you cannot, something is wrong anyway, and your lifestyle needs an honest self-assessment.

Living expenses include all regular monthly expenses such as mortgage or rent, utilities, car payment, groceries; plus dollars you set aside in a separate short-term savings plan for periodic expenses such as clothing, insurance premiums, vacations, Christmas, and monthly budget surprises. If you still have consumer debts, your living expenses should also include dollars committed to debt elimination. (This is why, if your consumer debt load is heavy, you may not be able to start at 10 percent of net income for your long-range savings program. But start somewhere, and increase it as rapidly as you can until you have reached the 10-10-80 allotment.)

IT REALLY WORKS!

The "pay yourself first" strategy works! If you have not yet implemented it in your own personal finances, I heartily encourage you to make it one of your immediate financial goals. Then continue the strategy for as long as you earn income. And whenever extra income comes your way, try to designate a good portion of it to savings and investment.

Like Gary and Nicole and thousands of others, you can experience the freedom of knowing that you are better prepared for the emergencies, opportunities, and golden years that lie ahead.

TAKING ACTION

M
A
N
T
A
L
K

☐ *Within the next three days, go to a library or newsstand and copy the toll-free number of a money market fund. Call the fund and ask any questions you have about how the fund works and whether it offers an automatic transfer from your checking account. Request a prospectus and application.*

☐ *Within the same three days, determine what dollar amount you will designate to long-term savings every month. When the money market fund application arrives, fill it out and mail it within three days.*

☐ *Review your monthly budget and spending patterns. Can you conform your budget to the 10-10-80 Plan? If not yet, how close do you come to it? By what date will you be able to follow the 10-10-80 Plan?*

PART THREE

Making the Most of Your Marriage

**Understanding
and meeting
a woman's
special needs**

**LOVING THE
WOMAN IN
YOUR LIFE**

*Love seeks one thing only: the
good of the one loved. It leaves
all the other secondary things
to take care of themselves. Love,
therefore, is its own reward.*
THOMAS MERTON

There once was a man who
searched all his life for riches, at
great personal expense and sacri-
fice. His search for a mystical diamond mine took him across the
country, throughout the hemi-
sphere, around the world. He
knew that if only he could find
that diamond mine, he'd be
happy and fulfilled.

But he never found those
riches, and he died a penniless,
tired-out, embittered old man—
unaware that all the while his
own property sheltered the richest diamond mine in the world.

Sometimes we men are like
that. Those of us who are married
or engaged often do not stop to
realize how "rich" we are.

Think of it: God brings a priceless creation into our lives, and for some unexplainable reason she finds us lovable. She's willing to give of herself to us, to invest the rest of her life as a partner with us in the adventures that will come our way.

We enter into the union with a commitment to give of ourselves to her. We will love her, cherish her, minister to her needs, and be her best friend.

Yet, once we've come down from the initial ecstasies of newlywed love, we tend to go our own way emotionally, so focused on our careers and pursuits and personal needs that we don't appreciate the priceless treasure we have in our own homes.

In the years since the publication of my book *The Total Man,* I've received invitations to women's seminars and luncheons to share the male perspective on life. I always have to confess to these women that I'm still trying to figure out just what the male perspective is, for I'm still a student of life and probably always will be. But I share what I know, and what I think I know, and the women seem to appreciate any help they can get in understanding the men in their lives.

On several of these occasions I've asked the audience to give me just five more minutes of their time and thought, then had each woman write down several of their greatest emotional and relational needs they wish their men understood better.

Each time I do this, I strike a nerve. Usually I hear self-conscious laughter as several women turn to their friends and say something like "I don't think I have enough paper to write all of mine." But then they begin writing, and a new intensity comes over the room.

Why do they enjoy this five-minute exercise? I think they are being given an opportunity to express to a member of the male gender something that has

M
A
N
T
A
L
K

been stirring deep within their souls. They are hoping that somehow, sometime, some way, the frustrations they are writing about will be passed along to their men.

One woman's comment typifies the kind of responses I received:

> *I wish my husband were less preoccupied, less caught up in the routine of life. I need him to make our love a two-way commitment in which he is just as interested in understanding and meeting my needs as I am in understanding and meeting his.*

Understanding and meeting her needs. Was that part of my wedding vows?

Maybe not in those exact words. But when I promised to love Kathy, that is precisely what my words meant to her: *I commit myself to understanding, appreciating, and meeting your unique needs as a person.* She made the same commitment to me. And when you really think about it, that's what lasting love is all about. It's an action, not a feeling. An ongoing act of the will, not just a fleeting sensation of the loins.

Can you imagine the power of this kind of selfless love when it is given and returned consistently in a marriage? It grows! It lasts! That's how one marriage can stay on solid ground while others fall apart. And why a man and woman in their eighties can look at each other with an energetic twinkle and say honestly, "We're more in love now than ever!" They've discovered the principle of lasting love: *Understanding, appreciating, and meeting the needs of the other.*

Toward that goal, let me share with you a distillation of the most universal personal needs the women listed.

THE NEED FOR LOVE

I need to see by his actions and hear from his lips that he still values me more than anything else in his life. I long to see the tenderness, the glint in his eye, the respect he gave me in the early years.

All of us need to give and receive love, but often it is the *expression* of that love that distinguishes the male psyche from that of the female.

We men tend to be satisfied that our wives still love us if we don't see any evidence to the contrary. If she gets that meal on the table, keeps up with the housework, smiles when she talks, and isn't obviously angry with us, we assume that all's okay in the love department.

And we assume that she thinks the same way. We reason, *I'm providing a good portion of the income, am I not? I don't beat you; I get you gifts on Valentine's Day and your birthday; and I talk nice to you. Unless I tell you otherwise, of course I love you.*

We may be content if our wives tell us, "I love you" once a month. They, on the other hand, need to hear it every day. To them a genuine "I love you" affirms the fact that they are number one in someone's life, that someone stands with them through the bad times as well as the good.

Saying the words often is our first challenge. Saying them honestly is the second. To be meaningful, our words must be consistent with our attitudes and actions. "I love you" will mean nothing if we proceed to be self-absorbed, cold, dictatorial, or demeaning. She needs to hear it, then see it in action.

THE NEED FOR
PERSONAL SIGNIFICANCE

I need for him to understand my desire to do something positive with the skills the Lord has given me. I need to interact with other adults, to use my brain, to make a difference in my world.

God created every human being with an inner need to identify and pursue a mission in life—a mission that matters.

We examined this for our own lives when we discussed the importance of "believing in what we are doing." Identifying and moving forward with our purpose in life is key to our personal success, fulfillment, and significance.

Our wives have the same inner drive. Until just a few years ago, however, our culture tended to assume that every woman's sense of mission and personal significance was motherhood and housewifery. A woman who pursued her mission outside the home was considered selfish and overly ambitious.

Fortunately, that thinking has changed a bit. We men are gradually acknowledging that a woman's sense of purpose and mission does not necessarily have to be tied to our own mission. Just as we need our wives' backing as we pursue our mission in life, so they deserve our full moral support when it comes to identifying and fulfilling the mission God has given them.

We need to qualify that, however. In society's flirtation with the more radical side of liberation, there has been a notable tendency to look with disdain upon women who have chosen child rearing and homemaking as their full-time personal mission.

This is not only unfair, it is short-sighted. Whether a woman pursues this mission full-time or after working hours, it's difficult to think of a more significant contribution to our world than to love and nurture children into responsible, caring, young adults. Good parenting is a mission to which we men should be equally committed. Our pursuits of corporate profits and career advancement pale in comparison to the significance of preparing children for responsible adulthood.

At the same time, if a woman has a deep-down yearning to get out and work, go to school, teach, start a business, or do volunteer work, it is only selfish and short-sighted of us not to encourage and stand behind her.

Do you know what gives your wife a sense of significance—the inner knowledge and excitement that her life is making a difference? If she hasn't verbalized it clearly for you, encourage her to do so. Ask her to imagine herself at age ninety, looking back on her life. What three major things will she feel best about having accomplished? Then ask her what you can do to help her make it happen.

Never put down or treat lightly her desire to be significant. This is a deeply held, universal need, and the loving husband will do everything possible to help her identify and pursue that special mission in life.

THE NEED FOR SECURITY

I need a solid sense of security. Economically, I need for him to consider me an equal partner when it comes to financial and career decisions. Relationally, I need to know that our love is growing deeper and that we're in it for life.

What wise and honest person does not admit to this need?

Isn't the need for economic security one of the reasons we all work so hard each day, put up with demands from bosses and customers, sock money away in savings and investments, and put a roof over our heads and locks on our doors? We want to build buffers between ourselves and personal disaster.

If there's a difference between men and women, it's in how we may go about building a sense of economic security. We men think often of improving our lot, or trying our hand at something new, or finding that perfect scheme that will make us richer, stronger, wiser. For those rewards we're often willing to risk a temporary setback or even a major catastrophe—just to know we tried.

Our wives, though, lean toward the conservative when it comes to speculation and grandiose dreams. When we come home excitedly to share our idea for quitting the job and starting our own business, she wonders about little things like how we're going to pay the mortgage, car payment, utilities, and food. In most cases she would rather move along steadily, secure and solvent, than risk the savings account for a new venture. Economic security is important to her. The loving husband needs to exercise tenderness whenever he thinks of uprooting the status quo.

Just as important in her sight is relational security. It's as though God gifted women with an uncanny perception that men do not have: the ability to discern when an important relationship is not as good as it could be. To us, the marriage may be fine if there are no obvious problems. But to her, the absence of problems does not necessarily mean the relationship is an intimate one. She needs to see in us an ongoing, daily affirmation of the love we once pledged to her. Which leads us to . . .

THE NEED FOR INTIMACY

Where has the passion gone in our marriage? Not just the physical passion . . . I'm talking about the things that made us so special in the early days—the personal attention, the stimulating conversation, the sparkle in the eyes, the courtesy and respect, the close friendship, the ongoing romance.

It's not that we have a bad marriage. We've just let careers, stresses, children, and everyday life preoccupy us and take away the specialness that attracted us to each other in the first place.

This woman summarized in two paragraphs the frustration that seems to be common among many married women: *Where has the passion gone? I know this isn't Camelot, but I need the ongoing intimacy that assures me our love is growing, not fading.*

Intimacy is vital to all of us, but again our women are usually more honest in expressing the need.

Intimacy is staying *focused* on your relationship, the most important priority in your life.

It is mutual secrets and very private jokes. The sharing of personal dreams. The sexual embraces that signify two becoming one.

Intimacy is listening. It is unhurried, in-depth communication where each seeks to know, affirm, and encourage the other.

It is admiration shared by loving eye contact.

It is a spirit that conveys, "I would rather be with you than with anyone else."

It is the security of knowing, beyond the shadow of doubt, that there is one very special person who cares for you, wants to know you, wants to affirm and encourage you, wants to help you reach your potential, loves you in spite of yourself, desires you sexually, and would give his life for you.

Intimacy is priceless to her because it is what drew the two of you together in the first place. It signifies that you are just as enamored with her now as you were then, that you consider her the most delightful, important, special person in your whole world, bar none.

And be honest: Wouldn't you like to know that she feels the same way about you?

If you detect that this level of intimacy is missing from your marriage, let me encourage you to take the initiative to restore it. Start with the eyes: Begin looking her in the eyes again when you talk to her and when she talks to you. Let your eyes convey the same kind of gentle admiration you showed for her while you were dating.

Then, dedicate yourself to helping meet her special need for physical, emotional, and spiritual intimacy. The next few chapters will provide some practical ideas to get you started.

THE NEED FOR POSITIVE SELF-ESTEEM

With all the forces in the world that tear us down, I need someone in my corner who will build me up. Sometimes my husband makes little verbal digs at

me, and he doesn't realize how much it hurts.
Most of the time, though, he just doesn't bother
to encourage me or let me know I'm a winner.

In their excellent book *Building Your Mate's Self-Esteem*, Dennis and Barbara Rainey write that "self-esteem is either the crippler or the completer of the marriage relationship. . . . Your mate's self-esteem will either hinder or enhance his ability to learn, make decisions, take risks and resolve conflicts with you and others. It will either restrain him or refuel him."[1]

And for those of us who go straight to the bottom line: Positive self-esteem is vital to one's happiness. With it, life is an adventure. Without it, life is a dismal effort to endure another day.

In today's world, the loving husband cannot assume that his wife maintains a healthy self-esteem day in, day out. She may have flashbacks to a hostile upbringing in which she was often told she didn't measure up. She may be struggling at her job, or with her personal mission in life. Perhaps a valued relationship has gone sour.

And maybe, just maybe, the most important man in her life has not given her many recent indications that she is gifted, talented, or worthy of his deepest respect.

It is not realistic to presume that we can be totally responsible for our spouse's self-esteem, just as we cannot be totally responsible for her sense of security or significance. But as her pledged life partner committed to doing everything we can to bring her joy and fulfillment, we can and must be alert to opportunities to help her feel good about herself.

Several years ago I developed a simple acrostic to help remind me to take better initiative in this important area of Kathy's life. The word is *CARE*:

C: *Compliment her.*
A: *Admire her.*
R: *Respect her.*
E: *Encourage her.*

Sometimes these steps are verbal; they are always attitudinal. And *CARE* requires me to get my mind off myself and find something about that beautiful person that I can sincerely compliment, admire, respect, and encourage. The fun part is that these action steps soon began coming naturally, for once I began opening my eyes I found so much to admire and respect in her that genuine *CARE* has flowed almost daily ever since!

It doesn't take long, once a woman receives this kind of *CARE,* for her to begin returning the favor. Then you have two partners actively building each other's self-esteem as each takes initiative to convey admiration and respect for the other. And when that's a regular part of your marriage, your love and commitment to each other will reach heights you may never have imagined possible.

When you come right down to it, meeting the four previous "needs" we discussed in this chapter goes a long way toward building the self-esteem of a woman. The husband who develops his talent for expressing love, encouraging personal significance, building a sense of security and creating intimacy will find that in many cases his wife's need for positive self-esteem is already being met. *CARE,* if not already in action, will be icing on the cake.

TAKING ACTION

☐ *Starting today, take the initiative to say "I love you" to your special lady at least once each*

*day. If you're married, say it again at night
before the two of you drift off to sleep.*

☐ *Ask her to imagine herself at age ninety, looking back on her life. What three dreams will
she feel best about having accomplished?
Then ask her what you can do to help her
make those dreams happen.*

☐ *Memorize the CARE acrostic for building your
wife's self-esteem. Today, say or do something
to:*
__Compliment her
__Admire her
__Respect her
__Encourage her.

M

A

N

T

A

L

K

Overcoming six common barriers to good communication

WHY MEN DON'T TALK TO THEIR WIVES

Strides in communication now permit us to talk with people around the globe, but cannot bridge the ever-widening gaps within our own families.
GLORIA FRANCE

"Tom doesn't talk to me nearly enough," Diana told me after I had spoken at a women's breakfast. "Sometimes I feel like we have a big guessing game going on in our marriage. I need for him to take the lead in communication because if I always do it I come off like the nagging wife."

"Tell me why communication is important to you," I asked her.

Diana thought for a moment. "Well, to avoid misunderstandings and to clear up those that have already happened," she replied. "I guess most of all, just to know Tom loves me enough to listen and open up with me. But he usually seems preoccupied."

Are you like Tom? I know I tend to be.

God created humans to be interactive creatures. He gave us sight and sound and touch to convey and receive messages from one another. He gave us the mental capacity to formulate those messages in meaningful and creative ways. And he gave us souls so that we might convey our thoughts in ways that love, uplift, and edify.

But over time, an interesting phenomenon has taken place. In long-term relationships between men and women, the female of the species seems to have embraced the art of ongoing communication, making it an integral part of her total personhood. The male, on the other hand, has let meaningful communication become a lost art.

Like Diana, our wives long for that good, loving, conversation with us. Like Tom, we often find silence or surface communication more comfortable. Why?

Well, let's be honest with ourselves.

1. COMMUNICATION TAKES EFFORT.

Good communication can be hard work. And please, we've had an exhausting day. Our wives can't possibly appreciate the fact that the boss, the customer, and the employee all dumped on us this afternoon. We've been communicating-for-survival all day, and we deserve a break. Keep the kids out of our face. Do something else for awhile. We're entitled to some quiet.

WHAT ABOUT *HER* DAY?

Whenever I'm smarting from a tough day, I have to remember that Kathy's boss, customer, and employee may have dumped on her that day, too.

She may have experienced a heartbreaking incident that she needs to share. What makes my case so special that I can cut off any meaningful communication for the evening? We're partners here.

The tough days are when we need to help each other the most. Your wife needs to talk. You need to talk too, though you may not feel like it. But give yourselves some time to unwind, to get alone. Then ask about each other's day. And listen.

2. WE ALLOW TOO MANY DISTRACTIONS.

We let too many other demands pull our attention from quality interaction with our wives and children. Unintentionally, sure. But how many quality one-on-one times with your spouse or kids have been pushed aside by the workload, the TV schedule, the household chores, or the church or civic committee?

IT'S A MATTER OF PRIORITIES.

With all the distractions around you, you'll need to continually ask yourself what's more important, your life's partner or the workload? Your God-ordained relationship or the TV set? It's a decision we made when we met her at the altar, and we need to live by it now. Aside from our personal walks with God, there is nothing—absolutely nothing—that deserves precedence over our commitment to love and honor our wives.

3. WE DON'T WANT ANY SUDDEN EXPLOSIONS.

If we talk about this problem now we're likely to start an argument. Oh, please, not tonight.

Have you ever ventured into meaningful conversation with your wife only to have it backfire?

We all have. We attempted to address a problem, or to share what we thought was loving, wise advice, but she took it wrong. It may have been her week-before, or maybe it was our week-before, but our egos still sting from the experience and we're not about to let it happen again.

BAN THE BOMB

One of the keys to good communication is to not live in fear of disagreement. If things are that tenuous in your relationship, it's indicative of the need for better communication in the first place.

I've observed many marriages in which the husband subscribed to the philosophy that "the less we talk, the less friction there'll be, so I'd better not bring this up . . . ." All the while, the tension would build inside both husband and wife. Then, suddenly, *EXPLOSION!* One minor incident would detonate a childish shouting match, all because things weren't dealt with as they occurred.

Don't let your marriage become a time bomb. In chapter 13, "Fighting the Good Fight," we will focus on this crucial area.

4. WE'VE FORGOTTEN HOW TO TALK.

It's incredible but true. In the years since the courtship, when we could look into her eyes and talk about everything in heaven and earth, many of us have forgotten how to carry on a meaningful conversation.

A marriage counselor friend once told me of a husband who announced proudly, "We've never had an argument in our lives."

"How have you accomplished that?" my friend asked.

"We just don't talk," the wife replied.

Either from laziness or abandoned communication skills, this couple had limited their conversations to the weather and topics of similar significance. As a result, their union was dull and lifeless, and, according to my friend, both individuals were just plain boring to be around.

MARRIAGE'S THIRD DEADLIEST SIN

Next to abuse and infidelity, the greatest sin we can commit in marriage is to let the relationship become shallow and boring.

I know one couple in their late fifties whose children have flown from the nest. Over the decades of their marriage this couple has rarely ventured beyond surface communications: "I wonder what our weather will be like today." Or "I saw John this morning—he said Ellen may have to go into the hospital."

It would not be inaccurate to describe this marriage as an existence rather than a relationship. They'll stay together because they don't want to upset anything at this point in their lives, but the romance, adventure, and depth of ministry toward one another departed long ago.

In our next chapter, "The Manly Art of Good Communication," you'll find some suggestions to help you rediscover the art of meaningful conversation with the most important person in your life.

5. WE'VE BECOME SELF-ABSORBED.

Good communication is a two-way proposition. Selfish communication is one-way. And I'm convinced that the latter has become an epidemic.

You see it when you've listened empathetically to a friend, but when you start to share from your heart his eyes glaze over and he wraps up the conversation.

You see it when you've needed empathy, and your friend constantly changes the subject to his own situation.

You've experienced it. You know how much it hurts.

But you've also done it. All of us have. At work, at home, at church, listening is harder than talking. So we talk and think we're communicating.

Selfish communication is the trademark of the self-absorbed individual. It's one-way, me-first, my-story-tops-your-story. It says I'm worth listening to, but you're not.

LISTEN . . . JUST LISTEN

Make it a point to listen. Just this once, don't chime in with your opinion, your situation, your story. Look your special lady in the eye and hear what she's saying. Nod your head to acknowledge that you're with her. Ask questions to clarify and probe deeper. Take her hand in yours to show you care.

When you take this radical step, you'll discover something: Two-way conversation is rewarding. You'll learn things about this special person you never knew before. You'll find it fascinating that someone would trust you with her innermost thoughts. It *is* more blessed to give than to receive.

We're all self-absorbed to some degree. We've been that way since Eden.

But we don't have to continue that way. With God's help, we can become more others-focused than self-focused. And as we do, our spouses will begin to feel a deeper sense of partnership with us. When we communicate, consistently, that we really care about their needs, we will grow together in intimacy and mutual affirmation.

6. WE FEAR REVEALING THE REAL "ME."

What if she spots a weakness in me, or an area I'm not really too sure about? Even worse, what if she's right and I'm wrong?

This fear is so subtle, yet very much a part of the male rationale for silence. Perhaps it's the way we were raised, or a defense mechanism we've developed to survive the shark-infested waters of corporate life. We've learned that it's better to keep our mouths closed and appear foolish than to open our mouths and remove all doubt.

So we hesitate to venture beyond our conversational comfort zones. Even with our wives, we don't want to risk confirmation of our inadequacies or insecurities.

SHOW HER THE REAL YOU

If you're hesitant to delve deeply in thoughtful conversation because it might reveal shallowness or inadequacy, remember: We all must start somewhere! But we must start.

Such hesitation has no place in the genuine love relationship, for love encompasses an all-out, two-way trust. Since I love Kathy and she loves me, I must trust her with my feelings and ideas. I must trust that she will not reject or ridicule me because of my obvious weaknesses or inconsistencies. We're committed to building each other, not tearing each other down.

Do our wives know the real men inside their husbands? We have nothing to fear, men, in taking the initiative to reveal ourselves in conversation. Total, trusting honesty can only enliven your laughter, enrich your intimacy, and deepen the quality of your love for each other.

YOU'RE NOT ALONE

"Wow," one husband in his early forties exclaimed to me over lunch at a men's retreat. "You really nailed me with every one of those reasons why men don't communicate with their wives."

I chuckled, because I have personally been guilty on all charges. "You're not alone," I told my friend. "My beautiful wife can tell you that I still struggle with most of them myself."

It's true . . . rediscovering the lost art of communication is a life-long challenge for many men. But let me share something to motivate you to give it all you've got: *It's worth it.*

In my personal struggle to overcome the "strong, silent" image of manhood that has been popular with my generation, I've discovered that good communication with my special woman has a way of rejuvenating me.

With the sharing of experiences and ideas comes a refreshing burst of energy. The interaction relieves tensions by confirming that all's okay on the home front, that my life's partner is in my corner, that our problems are really minor in light of the big picture.

We men need communication just as much as our wives do.

And even more importantly, God has brought us into marriage not just to meet our needs, but so that we can meet the needs of another person who is priceless in his sight. We've been given the privilege and responsibility of ministering to this special woman on the deepest, most intimate level through unselfish interaction that says, "You're special to me. I care. I value our moments together over anything else in life."

TAKING ACTION

☐ *Review the six reasons why many men have trouble communicating with their wives. What areas do you think your wife would say are troublesome spots for you? Why?*

☐ *In the left column, rank the following items 1 through 6 in order of your personal priorities. In the right column, rank the same items 1 through 6 according to how your wife would say you actually live them.*

My Priorities .... How My Wife Would Rank
My Priorities

——— .... Hobbies..................... ———

——— .... Time with God .... ———

——— .... Career/Work Load............ ———

——— ....Intimacy with Wife .... ———

——— .... TV Time..................... ———

——— ....Intimacy with Kids............. ———

☐ *What one thing will you begin doing today to demonstrate to her that good communication is important to you?*

Restoring
the joy of
meaningful
conversation

THE MANLY
ART OF GOOD
COMMUNI-
CATION

To think justly, we must under-stand what others mean.
WILLIAM HAZLITT

"They can't be married—they're *talking!*"

It's an old joke among restaurant goers, but if you look around the room next time you're dining out, odds are you'll agree that there is some underlying truth to the punchline.

Watch the couples at their tables. Which ones are talking animatedly, looking into each other's eyes, enjoying their conversations? Then, which are passively focused on their plates, sharing little eye contact, talking only to comment on the food or to share a brief tidbit of news?

If you were so bold as to stroll to each table and ask how long each couple has known each other, chances are the longer a couple has been together, the duller their communication patterns have become.

If they're dating or engaged, they can't get enough of each other's thoughts. They're talking about each other's upbringing, values, plans, and dreams.

But if they've been married for awhile, they've already covered all that. The big topic of the evening is, "How's your salmon?"

Fortunately, not all marriages turn out this way. I hope yours hasn't. That woman you love still has a deep, passionate need for you to talk together like you used to. You have the same need, though you may have buried it under a pile of other priorities.

But as marriage counselors will confirm, many husbands aren't very good at talking with their wives on a meaningful level. We pride ourselves on being good communicators in our work, but then we come home to people we no longer need to impress. We let down, switch into neutral. Hence, the common lament of frustrated wives everywhere, "My husband won't talk to me!"

So here's a guaranteed way to rise above the crowd and be a rare gem to her: Brush up on those communication skills and take consistent initiative to keep the lines open and flowing.

WHAT IS GOOD COMMUNICATION?

The opposite of silence—merely talking—is not necessarily good communication. There are probably as many perpetual talkers in divorce courts today as there are silent couples. Good, meaningful communication meets two important criteria.

GOOD COMMUNICATION
GOES BEYOND THE MUNDANE.

Or as someone has aptly stated, "Weak minds talk about people; mediocre minds talk about events; but great minds talk about ideas."

Why are people and the weather so easy to talk about? Because they're nonthreatening. They don't require much thought, effort, or risk. People and events make good topics for occasional discussion, but families who limit their conversations to them can become boring gossips.

Use people and events as springboards to more significant subjects. Discussing *ideas* is what stretches our minds and helps our loved ones grow into effective thinkers and conversationalists. Ideas cause us to transcend everyday pettiness and rise to a higher plane of thoughts and dreams. Ideas draw people closer together as they ask, then answer, questions such as:

"What do you think about . . . ?"

"What if . . . ?"

"I wonder why . . . ."

GOOD COMMUNICATION IS TWO-WAY.

William Hazlitt wrote that "the art of conversation is the art of hearing as well as of being heard." How easy it is to expound on our own knowledge and opinions, but to listen with only half of one ear as the other person speaks! Ambrose Bierce has provided a perceptive, tongue-in-cheek definition of conversation as too many of us experience it:

> *Conversation, n. A fair for the display of the minor mental commodities, each exhibitor being too intent upon the arrangement of his own wares to observe those of his neighbor.*

Do you recognize this in yourself or someone you know?

The art of listening is an essential but oft ignored element of loving communication. To listen means focusing on the verbal and physical expressions of the speaker, hearing her complete message, and assimilating the message so that you understand both the message and how she feels about it. If neither the message nor feeling are clear, the good listener will ask questions to clarify.

In the mid 1970s psychologists coined a term for selfish communication: "egospeak." Some have since devised other names for it, but none paint a more vivid picture. The word means just what it says: that some people simply enjoy listening to themselves more than to anyone else.

Egospeak is thinking of what you're going to say next while another person is talking to you. Constantly shifting the conversation to your own stories or opinions. Taking and holding a deep breath so you can jump in on the other person's last word. Topping the other person's story.

Watch—and listen—carefully. You'll spot egospeak in almost every conversation these days. If not corrected, egospeakers can quickly become boring clods whom no one wants to be around.

STARTING A GOOD CONVERSATION

Once you are committed to go beyond the mundane and to listen unselfishly, the key to initiating good communication is simple: Ask questions and listen.

With just a little practice, you'll soon learn which types of questions lead to the most fascinating types of conversation. "How are you feeling?" inevitably evokes either a "Fine" or an organ recital. "Do you have choir practice tonight?" encourages only a yes or no. End of discussion.

The principle of asking good questions is to ask *thought questions* that require more than a yes-or-no answer. These will ask a person how he *feels* about a topic, event, philosophy, or problem.

To help you get started, we've prepared a number of questions that every husband and wife should try to discuss together frequently. (Wives, I know many of you are "reading in." Be cooperative with your husband's efforts here—it might be a milestone in your marriage! And don't hesitate to ask him the same questions yourself.)

QUESTIONS TO TALK ABOUT WITH YOUR WIFE
OUR MARRIAGE

1. What are some of the greatest lessons we've learned since we've been married?

2. How has marriage enriched your life? Mine?

3. Are there areas where you feel I should be providing stronger initiative?

4. Do you feel I spend enough quality time with you and the children? Would you help me think through how I can better manage my time to do so?

5. How can I be more sensitive to your personal needs?

6. Next time we can get away, what would you like to do together?

7. Do you feel I'm open enough in communicating and expressing love to you and the children? Would you help me think through some practical steps I can take to do better?

8. How has God been speaking to us during the past year?

9. What rules should we set up now to assure that our disagreements can be resolved amicably?

10. Do you like the general direction in which our marriage is headed? What do you like? What would you like to see us do better?

11. What would you like to see us accomplish together this next year? Five years? By the time we retire?

12. If you knew we could not fail, what one thing would you like to see us attempt together?

13. Would you like to spend more or less time together with other married couples?

14. What are some areas of your life you'd like to develop? How can I help you?

15. How can we encourage each other more?

OUR SEX LIFE

1. If there were one thing you would want to convey to husbands about a woman's sexuality, what would it be?

2. What can I do during the day to help prepare you for fulfilling sex in the evening?

3. Are there any problems in our sexual relationship that you would like us to talk about?

4. Do you have sexual fantasies that you'd like us to try together?

5. I realize that our preferences and desires may change from time to time. How can I learn to read your signals so I can respond and satisfy you most fully?

M
A
N
T
A
L
K

OUR MONEY

1. What do you think our financial goals should be for the next three years? The next ten years?

2. Do you feel financially secure? If not, what are some things we can be doing to help you feel secure?

3. What are some improvements we can make in the way we manage our money?

4. Are you content with the amount we're giving to charity? What church, organization, or needy individual could we help financially?

5. On what guidelines should we agree to help us keep spending under control?

6. How much should we be tucking away in savings each month? In long-term investments?

7. If we were retiring tomorrow, what life-style, location, and income level would you like to experience?

8. What things should we be doing to teach the children wise financial management?

OUR CHILDREN

1. What specific things can we do to show our children how much we love each other?

2. Do you feel I spend enough time playing and talking with them? Would you help me come up with some ways I can do better?

3. What specific things should we be doing to build positive self-esteem in each of the kids?

4. What are some positive ways we can encourage them:

to be unselfish?
to respect others?
to be responsible?
to be good stewards of their property and money?
to develop their skills?
to remain sexually pure?
to resist negative peer pressure?
to choose right over wrong?
to choose good friends?
to love, obey, and serve God?

5. How can we be more consistent and effective when it becomes necessary to discipline them?

6. What should be our policy to teach responsible use of the TV set?

7. What practical skills should we be teaching them that will equip them for living?

8. How can we teach them to be assertive without being obnoxious?

9. Are we doing a good job of modeling how a man and woman should love and respect one another? How can we do better?

10. What activities could we be doing together to stimulate family togetherness?

11. What have you enjoyed most about being the mother of our children?

OUR SPIRITUAL LIFE

1. Do you see areas of my spiritual walk that need improvement? Would you help me think of some specific things I could do to grow in my relationship with God?

2. What can I be doing better to encourage you in your spiritual journey?

3. What are some specific areas in which we need to trust God more?

4. As a couple, are we honoring and glorifying God by the way we live? By our talk? Our attitudes? How can we do better?

5. What did you read from the Bible this morning? What did it mean to you?

6. May I share with you something great that God taught me today?

7. What are at least ten blessings God has brought into our lives this past year?

8. Are we modeling a joyful, Christ-like life-style for our children? Does our walk match our talk?

9. How can I pray for you this week?

10. What do you think God would like us to do to help others know him better?

GENERAL

1. What's the best thing that happened to you today?

2. What do you think of . . . (a news item, etc.)?

3. How do you feel about . . . (a current philosophy or idea)?

4. What if . . . ?

5. What can we do for . . . (someone who's hurting, someone we love, etc.)?

6. What's one of your favorite memories from childhood? Junior high? High school? College? Our early years together?

7. What was one of your most embarrassing moments?

8. What do you appreciate most about your mom or dad? About my mom or dad?

9. What do you like most about your job? Our marriage? Being a mom? Our church? Our friends?

10. What are some of the most humorous things that have happened to you/me/us since we have known each other?

11. When you're ninety years old and looking back on your life, what three things would you most like to have accomplished?

TAKING ACTION

☐ *Think back on the conversations you've had with your wife during the past two weeks. Would you say that most of your discussions were about people and events, or about ideas?*

☐ *Select two questions from those suggested in this chapter and bring them up in conversation within the next twenty-four hours.*

☐ *This week, make a date for breakfast or lunch at a favorite restaurant. Prepare three or four questions from the suggested list and use them as conversation starters.*

M
A
N
T
A
L
K

FIGHTING THE GOOD FIGHT

The aim of argument, or of discussion, should not be victory, but progress. JOSEPH JOUBERT

Take two people
   One male, one female
   From totally different homes
   With different upbringing and
      experiences
   Created with different temper-
      aments
   And with emotional uniqueness
   With different likes and dislikes
   Each with some degree of inde-
      pendence
   And self-centeredness.

Join them together "till death do
us part"
   Put them in the same house
   With different tasks and
      responsibilities
   Working from a common budget
   Trying to agree upon common
      goals.

Despite a firm commitment of
love and loyalty to one another,

the fact that the husband and wife are two distinct people make some degree of conflict inevitable.

Disagreements will happen.

Rights will be stepped on.

Feelings will be hurt.

And there will be moments when the romantic dream will be shattered by the thought, *Why did I ever marry you, anyway?*

You've experienced it. I've experienced it.

It's all part of living with another human being. Especially if you're a male and she's a female of the opposite sex.

The important thing is that we not allow the inevitable disagreements to neutralize or destroy the most precious human relationship we could ever long for. If a rift is poorly managed and unresolved, it can only tear down the partnership, leading either to loveless coexistence or divorce due to "irreconcilable differences."

If managed properly, though, disagreements can actually serve as a proving ground to help us spot communication gaps and personal weaknesses that need improvement. The key word is *can.*

Managing such conflicts has not been a strong suit for most husbands. Those of us at executive or management levels may have received conflict resolution training for the job, but we've had a tough time transposing those skills to the most important relationship of our lives. As one thirtysomething woman shared at a wives' meeting, "Solving an argument with my husband is like negotiating with a brick wall. Either he clams up and hopes it all goes away, or he gets real stubborn and expects me to give in."

THE ROOT PROBLEM OF DIVORCE

Howard Markman, a psychologist with the University of Denver, has studied 150 couples for ten years in an attempt to learn how to prevent divorce. "Compared to women, men seem to have difficulty handling negative emotions and conflict," he reports. "Since they were little boys, men have negotiated around rules in games. They have not been socialized to handle unstructured conflict."

Markman states that the topics we argue about—money, sex, in-laws, intimacy—aren't the root problems that lead to divorce. Rather, "How a couple handles the conflict itself seems to be the biggest task."[1]

I have to agree. If I had to select one key that determines whether a couple will stay together and happy, it would be how they go about resolving the inevitable conflicts of married life. A married couple can have all the romance in the world, the greatest in-laws, perfect health and finances, all-American children, and even a personal commitment to God, but if they lack conflict resolution skills, their good marriage can come apart at the seams.

A FEW UNCOMFORTABLE MOMENTS

Do you allow conflict to destroy the intimacy between you and your wife? Or do you harness conflict to help make your marriage better?

I have to admit I've been one of those husbands who tend to become either sullen or stubborn when an argument comes along. My usual strategy is to wait it out until Kathy realizes the error of her ways, throws herself into my arms, and begs forgiveness.

And it's usually a long wait. For one thing, conflict resolution only happens that way on "The Young and the Restless." And at least half the time *I'm* the culprit who needs to realize the errors of *my* ways.

In real life, I'm having to learn how to swallow my blind pride and invest a few uncomfortable moments in working through disagreements face to face.

Has it been fun? Usually not. Sometimes the making up part is, but only when preceded by hard work and some time for hurt feelings to heal.

Has it been worth it? Always. I've learned that if I'll only come out of my shell and do my part of the partnership, conflict *can* serve as a strengthening agent in our marriage.

One valuable tool Kathy and I have developed over the years is a set of rules to guide us through those skirmishes. Like the Geneva Convention, we've agreed on these guidelines ahead of time so if we see battle lines forming, we'll fight by the rules in order to attack the *problem*, not the *person*.

Our guidelines have proven invaluable in helping us face up to our problems and work them out as calmly as possible. From practice, we've even learned to head off many potential conflicts before they occur. The most important benefit, though, is that we've been able to achieve a genuine sense of closure and forgiveness on every offense to date so grievances do not accumulate, plant roots, and kill us slowly from the inside.

GUIDELINES FOR A GOOD FIGHT

If you and your wife have never agreed in advance on some guidelines for a "good" fight, we heartily recommend that you do. They'll help assure that conflicts won't poison your relationship. To help you get started, here are some of the guidelines that have served us well.

1. *The offended person will state the problem in a non-accusatory, loving manner.* Some Marriage Encounter facilitators suggest a wording like this:

"When *(an event)*, I feel *(fearful, angry, hurt, etc.)* because *(positive statement about your relationship)*."

Let's try a specific example:

> *"When you don't call me when you're going to come home late, I feel worried and upset because I can't imagine how terrible it would be if something happened to you."*

If your wife said that to you, would you be offended? Probably not. Would you sense her love, even though she's bringing up a point of contention? Probably so. That's the key to this statement. Let me suggest that you and your wife memorize it and practice it on a variety of fictional scenarios. Then agree to implement it when a real offense comes along.

2. *We will determine whether the problem is an offense or a misunderstanding.* In our example above, the late spouse might have a perfectly good explanation. If he was stuck in traffic or had a flat tire, the "offended" party simply misunderstood. It's a misunderstanding, not an offense, and the "offended" party apologizes.

However, if the late spouse was downright negligent in calling home, this is an offense on his part. The "offender" apologizes.

This noninflammatory technique can defuse many potential conflicts before they have a chance to erupt into a full-scale battle. But to help assure that even the toughest conflicts are dealt with in love, further guidelines are in order.

3. *Never, never in public.* Since we aren't auditioning for the soap operas (we're neither "Young" nor "Restless"), this disagreement is nobody's business but ours. We will afford each other the dignity of waiting until we can be alone.

4. *We will try to remain calm.* Angry voices will only exacerbate the problem. So we'll make a point to say, "We've got a problem here. Let's take a moment to gather our thoughts, then sit down and talk it through."

5. *We will affirm our love for each other.* Even though we may not feel very loving (or lovable) at the moment, we'll sit side by side, hold hands, and affirm our love verbally: "I disagree with you (or, "I'm mad at you") right now, but I love you and I want to work with you to resolve this."

6. *We will try to give the other the benefit of the doubt.* Unless the other person admits otherwise, he meant well. He was trying as hard as he could to do the right thing.

7. *We will try to use "I" statements instead of "you" statements.* We will make observations, not accusations:

"YOU" (ACCUSATION)	→	"I" (OBSERVATION)
"You're insensitive!"	→	"I feel misunderstood."
"Will you shut up and listen?"	→	"I don't think we're communicating."
"You never pay attention to me!"	→	"I feel left out."
" . . . and then you started yelling . . ."	→	"It bothers me when we yell at each other."
"You broke my grandmother's pitcher!"	→	"I'm upset that the pitcher is broken."

8. *We will listen.* Egospeak is not allowed. We will remain quiet and attentive while the other speaks, speaking only to ask questions so we can fully understand why he feels the way he does.

9. *We will be open-minded to the possibility that we're wrong.* Defensiveness is always destructive. Our attitude will be, "Well, I may be wrong in this area. Let me tell you why I said what I did."

10. *We will avoid these statements:* "You *always . . .*" and "You *never . . . .*" If these generalizations were really true, they should have been discussed and forgiven when they first occurred. But since most likely they are not true, they have no place in a fair fight.

11. *We will not dredge up past, forgiven offenses.* Part of helping each other grow is to allow the other the freedom to make mistakes. If past offenses were forgiven, they must be forgotten.

12. *We will not stomp from the room.* Throwing a zinger over one's shoulder while stomping out of the room is a foul. If things get too hot, we'll stop for a breather by saying, "I need a few minutes to get my thoughts together. I don't want to say something hurtful in anger."

13. *We will bring closure to the issue.* To be honest, sometimes we'd rather be mad for a while. That's okay. But we won't leave the issue hanging, hoping it will somehow go away, only to have it build up inside us. After some cooling off time, we'll make sure all is discussed until agreement or compromise is reached. Then we'll ask, "What have we learned from all this? What can we do to prevent this from being a problem again?"

14. *We will be sure to ask forgiveness and to forgive.*
This is the most important part, for without it there
is no closure. If the other person has been offended,
we will say, "I'm sorry, Honey. I was wrong. Will you
please forgive me?" And the other will never fail to
grant it: "Yes, I forgive you. Will you please forgive
me?"

TIME WOUNDS ALL HEELS

One of the most well-intentioned but misleading myths of human relationships goes like this:
Time heals all wounds.

Don't believe it. Only closure and forgiveness can
heal wounds to the human spirit. Without genuine
forgiveness, time will simply give resentment more
opportunity to sink its roots deeper.

In spite of all the guidelines we try to follow for a
"good" fight, forgiveness is the one sure way to a
happy outcome. With it comes a release of all the
guilt, tension, and hurt feelings that could have poi-
soned the relationship. True forgiveness helps both
parties forget the past and move on with the positive
opportunities of life.

TAKING ACTION

☐ *Reflect on psychologist Howard Markman's*
statement, "Compared to women, men seem
to have difficulty handling negative emotions
and conflict." In your case, is Markman right?
Would your wife agree or disagree with him?
Why?

☐ *Think back. Is there a fight in your past for*
which you have not yet sought and granted
complete forgiveness? If so, take the steps
today to bring closure to the issue.

M

A

N

T

A

L

K

☐ *With your wife, read through and discuss how you will begin to implement the suggested "Guidelines for a Good Fight." Add some guidelines of your own.*

WHAT WIVES WISH THEIR HUSBANDS KNEW ABOUT SEX

*The man should give his wife
all that is her right as a married
woman, and the wife should do
the same for her husband . . .
do not refuse these rights to
each other.*
PAUL (1 Corinthians 7:3-5, TLB)

When I get to heaven, one of the questions I'm going to ask God is why he designed men and women so differently when it comes to the sex drive.

I mean, wouldn't he have made it a whole lot easier if he had designed women to desire sex as often as we do? If women were aroused as easily as we are?

I realize there are mitigating factors. A caring wife and mother has a few other things on her mind. There are times when she is just as sexually eager as we, but if something goes bump in the night or a small child lets out so much as a whimper, her desires may go on "hold" until all is at peace.

143

We men, on the other hand, can be very single-minded when it comes to sex. If the time is right, just mention the word, press the right button—and suddenly little else matters. Let the burglar take the TV set—we'll buy another one. Let the child whimper—it's good for him.

Thus we begin our subtle (sometimes not-so-subtle) attempt at seduction. And she responds in one of three ways: (1) she's eager to join in; (2) she's lukewarm, but goes along; (3) she has a headache.

So man's quest through the ages, right up there with answering the question, *"Why am I here?"* has been to find ways to increase the frequency of response Number One and reduce the frequency of responses Two and Three.

And through the ages, we've tried all kinds of tactics to make women as sensually eager as we are. Flowers. Dinner out. Gifts. Begging. You name it, we've tried it. One night it seems to work; the next night it doesn't. One night is like the fourth of July; the next night she'd rather crochet.

Has anyone figured this all out?

Well, sort of.

In one of the most brilliant discoveries of human history, sexuality experts have recently acknowledged that yes, men and women are different. (This discovery probably landed them a Nobel prize and a book deal.) But here's the important part: Since men and women are different, we tend to look at sex from different perspectives as well.

You and I already know what arouses the male libido. While a woman certainly is capable of spontaneous arousal through sight, thought, and touch, her sexuality tends to be more an integral part of her emotional and relational being. Cultural researcher

Shere Hite found that "most women interviewed enjoyed hugging, kissing, cuddling, closeness, and conversation as much as intercourse. Overall, intimacy was more important than orgasm."[1]

KEY #1:
A GREAT RELATIONSHIP

Thus, while men tend to believe the most vital sex organ is the penis, women believe the most vital sex organ—for both sexes—is *the mind*. If her relationship with you is one of ongoing love, intimacy, meaningful communication, and romance, her mind tells her all systems are "go" for sexual enjoyment. But if something is wrong in the marriage, her mind brings your advances to a screeching halt by shouting, *Wait a minute, Buster. There's something rotten in our relationship. It would be hypocritical for us to make love right now.*

For this reason, women generally agree that the key to great sex is a great relationship. The husband who takes the initiative to meet his wife's emotional and relational needs on a daily basis will receive a much more positive sexual response than the self-absorbed, noncommunicative husband whose sudden fits of passion seem to come from left field.

Women who emphasize that "a great relationship" is the number one key to sexual fulfillment usually hasten to add two other important factors: number two, an unselfish husband; and number three, a knowledgeable husband. Both are worth a closer look.

KEY #2:
AN UNSELFISH HUSBAND

The way a man goes about making love with his wife has an uncanny way of revealing the true nature of his everyday love for her.

One man may love his wife so much that, to him, the meeting of her sexual needs comes first. He's patient, gentle, loving, and skillful as he makes love in ways she has indicated are sensuous and meaningful to her.

Another man says he loves his wife, but once foreplay starts, it's "Beat the Clock." His selfishness or clumsiness (or both) relieves his passion within minutes, leaving her feeling used, frustrated, and unsatisfied.

Which wife do you think will be most eager for sex again?

If we remember that successful sex is the total quality of intimacy surrounding the relationship, we know the answer to the above question. The woman who senses the most generous spirit of love from her husband is the one who is the most fulfilled and will want to experience the closeness again soon.

The unselfish husband is patient and undemanding. He understands that his wife will not always desire sex whenever he does. He can hold and caress his wife without necessarily expecting sex to follow. This type of closeness is simply an act of intimacy that should be part of each day. If his wife knows that his hugs and caresses are given without obligation, just because he loves her, she can enjoy and return the intimacy because she isn't expected to always "shift gears" and respond with sexual passion.

He will also be patient amidst the challenge of trying to enjoy a passionate sexual relationship in a houseful of children. At times, the children may preoccupy her thoughts. At other times, the children are just plain *there*.

I was one of four brothers. Looking back, I realize that my dear mom and dad faced quite a challenge looking for those special moments of privacy. I'm sure my brothers and I caused more changes of plan than we'll ever know. But Mom and Dad did find discreet ways to keep the home fires burning, and now, happier-than-ever in their seventies, they are involved in the Marriage Encounter movement to help younger couples. They confide:

> *Finding a time for lovemaking became rather complicated. . . . Just when we thought everyone was settled for the night and we were enjoying candlelight and mood music, some little boy would cry out because of a bad dream or because he was lonesome or wanted a drink of water. [Author's Note: This obviously refers to one of my brothers.]*
>
> *Years later, when the boys were teenagers, they and their friends were in and around the house at all hours, playing music, keeping the refrigerator door well exercised, wanting to talk with us about something important. Privacy was a rare commodity.*
>
> *It required a lot of patience, perseverance, and scheming. . . . Sometimes now, with just the two of us at home, we actually miss the excitement of that extra element of challenge!*

We men have to be realistic and understand that the presence of children does not always lend itself to sexual spontaneity. But we can take initiative to help create the atmosphere for sexual love by planning ahead with our wives as much as possible, and by being patient and loving if our plans don't happen to come about.

When sexual togetherness does take place, the

unselfish husband is eager for his wife to experience joy and fulfillment. He takes the time to prepare himself and the surroundings. He shares in unhurried, generous foreplay. He does the things she likes and avoids the things she does not like. And when the act is completed he holds her, caresses and kisses her, tells her how great she is, and thanks her for the time of his life.

KEY #3:
A KNOWLEDGEABLE HUSBAND

The knowledgeable husband takes the time and initiative to learn his wife's sexual response patterns. What arouses her? What turns her off? What enhances the total sexual experience for her?

As we've already seen, a woman's sexual response begins with the total relationship. A crucial part of the relationship is good communication in which you become more knowledgeable about the unique sensual makeup of each other.

Several smart couples I know have begun this communication process by selecting a creative book on the subject. Then each spouse went through the book, writing comments in the margin for the other to see.

The more direct approach, of course, is to talk about your personal likes and dislikes. Questions such as the ones below might seem a bit bold at first, but you'll find that honest discussion can help make the act of love a more mutually satisfying experience:

> *"If there were one thing you'd like to convey to husbands about a woman's sexuality, what would it be?"*

> *"What do you enjoy most when we're making love?"*

M
A
N
T
A
L
K

"What would you like me to do during the day to help prepare you for intimacy in the evening?"

"What would you like me to do during foreplay and intercourse to make the experience as fulfilling as possible for you?"

"Do you have a sexual fantasy that you'd like us to try together?"

"I realize that preferences and desires may change from time to time. What has changed for you? What excites you now?"

Just as men have different erotic likes and dislikes, so do women, and it would be a mistake to assume that all women respond identically. However, there are several factors on which most women do agree.

BEFORE BED

Most women acknowledge they are more apt to respond favorably to a spirit of confident gentleness and romance, to cleanliness and good grooming, to favorite smells and neat, attractive clothing. Special touches such as soft background music, dim lighting, or candlelight can enhance the setting. Romantic precursors such as flowers or other gifts may get the mood going, but men should not fall into the pattern of bringing home such gifts only when hoping for sexual passion.

Sexual Adventure. Assuming that their men are meeting Key #1, "A Great Relationship," most wives also welcome a spirit of sexual adventure. One of the unnecessary sins of married love is to let sex become the same old routine. What have you always wanted to do together but been hesitant to suggest?

The best way to find out is to discuss it together some evening when the lights are low and the libido is high. If you've ever wondered what is meant by "stimulating conversation," you won't wonder much longer.

If you find yourself locked into a sort of sex-by-the-schedule routine (only at bedtime, only in your bed), do yourself a favor and break free once in awhile. See if you can clear the house for some daytime sex in another part of the house. Or let the family room carpet (complemented with a blanket, sheet, and fluffy pillows) serve as your bed after a fireside dinner together. As much as possible, let spontaneity rule when it comes to a time and place for sex.

A Night to Remember.   Several smart husbands I know arrange occasional X-rated nights with their wives away from the house. They'll agree on a date in advance, reserve a nice hotel room, arrange sitters for the kids. The whole week before is a romantic buildup with loving phone calls from work and intimate whispers at home. Then the husband and wife help each other select and pack favorite clothing, jewelry, and colognes; some like to take along candles, sparkling cider, and a portable cassette or CD player to help set the mood.

IN BED

Again, your best way of knowing what pleases your woman in bed is to ask her. She'll probably have some personal favorites and least-favorites to share with you.

Gentle, Unhurried Foreplay.   For most women, gentleness is the important watchword during foreplay. It implies an ongoing communication between the two of you as to what excites and what detracts from arousal. Gentleness excludes the wild grabbing of breasts and other erogenous areas, as well as the misplaced elbow. But it does include the generous use of your hands and lips in tender caresses of her body, with her guiding you verbally as to what excites her. As her level of pleasure increases, the pressure you apply can be gradually increased—but not at first. Enter foreplay with all the gentleness of word and touch that got you both there in the first place.

Every man should know about the clitoris, but many do not. This is a tiny, sensitive, erectile organ located at the front of the vulva. The clitoris is the female equivalent to the male's penis, which should tell you quite a bit about how it responds to proper stimulation. Though it does not ejaculate, it does become engorged through stimulation and some-what enlarged with sexual arousal, and it is the key to her orgasm.

According to sex therapists, few women like for men to fondle the clitoris right away. Without suffi-cient pre-arousal, the vulva and clitoris can be too sensitive to the touch, causing more discomfort than pleasure. That's one of the reasons unhurried, unself-ish foreplay is important to her, for when her clitoris is truly ready you are both in for a fun time.

The Slow, Loving Touch.   Practically every inch of the female body responds to the loving touch, but there are several erogenous zones that especially excite her. You can gently kiss her eyelids, ears, earlobes, lips, neck, breasts, tummy, and thighs. With your free hand you can *slowly and lovingly* caress her breasts, tummy, thighs, and pubic area.

By this time her clitoris will probably be ready for

gentle contact. A simple way to locate the clitoris is by placing your palm on her lower abdomen, fingers down, then sliding your hand downward until your middle finger descends over the vulva. With just a slight amount of pressure, you'll feel the stiffened shaft of the clitoris with the tip of your finger. If you have trouble finding it, have your wife guide your hand with hers.

Experience and communication will tell you just how much pressure and stimulation best suits her wishes. Many women want continued gentleness here; some prefer a firm, side-to-side stimulation by the finger or a combination of gentleness and firmness. One important note, however: Avoid continuing the same kind of manipulation over a length of time, as the clitoris can become numb, irritated, or oversensitive from too much of a good thing. Fondle it briefly, then leave it for awhile, then come back, then move on again.

Becoming One. There is only one proper time for the husband to insert his erect penis into the wife's vagina, and that is when she is ready for it. As her excitement builds, her natural lubricants will release into the vagina to help make intercourse comfortable for her. By allowing her to be the judge of the timing of entry, you will not risk pushing yourself upon her before she is physically or emotionally ready. When she senses that the time is right, she can guide you with her hand toward her vagina and position the penis for entry.

There has long been a myth hovering over the marriage bed that truly satisfying sex can only occur upon *simultaneous orgasm*—in which both partners reach orgasm at the same instant. The truth is that while simultaneous orgasm is indeed pleasant, it is not at all necessary for complete fulfillment, nor is it as probable as some would have us believe.

A more realistic and enjoyable goal in sexual intercourse is *mutual orgasm*—in which both husband and wife bring the other to that distinct sexual release. Gentle, unhurried foreplay on your part, plus a desire to try to bring her to climax before you reach orgasm, can help assure that she reaches this level of fulfillment.

Well-Chosen Words. Before, during, and after, well-chosen words can be an exciting part of the mounting rhapsody. As you stimulate each other, you can affirm by your words that you love her, that you love her body, that she is driving you wild. If, during foreplay, her handwork has brought you to the brink of orgasm too soon, you might tell her in an appreciative tone that she has brought you right to the edge. That's her cue to reduce the stimulation for a while, and you can use your simmer-down time to further caress and stimulate her. If you've already entered her, you can help stave off that glorious moment with another appreciative verbal cue, while pausing for a few seconds to lie still for a long kiss.

You might also want to agree ahead of time on a sensuous verbal cue your wife can give when she feels her orgasm coming on. Those well-chosen words will be music to your ears, for they are testimony that you have done your part well and are about to enjoy the pleasure of either simultaneous or mutual orgasm.

Afterglow. This is the time when she wants your tender assurances the most, perhaps more than any other time in your marriage. It's also the time when a depressing number of husbands roll over and fall asleep.

Don't minimize the importance of the afterglow, for to her it's as much a part of the love act as orgasm itself. Stay awake. Hold her close as you lie together in complete, unhurried luxury. Tell her how great it felt to be *one* with her. Bathe her in soft kisses as you thank her for sharing herself with you. Tell her again how much she turned you on. Let her know that you wouldn't have traded the last hour for anything else the world could offer.

LOVE IS PATIENT AND KIND

Of course, despite everything we Romeos try, there will still be those times when our wives do not feel up to sexual intimacy. Menstrual cycles, illness, fatigue, or pressing problems are legitimate reasons that we all need to understand. That's our chance to show the true quality of our love, the "patient, kind" love of 1 Corinthians 13 that "is not self-seeking" and "not easily angered."

And when you stop to think about it, maybe that's why God created us so differently in the first place—so that husband and wife would have daily opportunities to discover and appreciate the intricate uniqueness he has built into the other person. And so we can learn to love each other patiently, unselfishly—no matter what the circumstances.

TAKING ACTION

☐ *If your wife were reading this chapter by herself, how do you think she would grade you, from 1 to 10, in these three areas:*
   ___*We have a great marriage relationship.*
   ___*He's an unselfish husband.*
   ___*He's a knowledgeable husband.*

☐ *Make a mental list of specific things you'd like to do better to create an atmosphere for sexual intimacy with your wife.*

☐ *If you haven't talked together recently about your sexual relationship, pick an appropriate time and ask, "Could I ask you some questions to help me understand you better?" Then discuss the questions suggested in this chapter.*

Never let the courtship end. Keep romancing her as if you were trying to win her heart for the very first time.

101 WAYS TO TELL HER "I LOVE YOU"

Love sought is good, but given unsought is better.
WILLIAM SHAKESPEARE

Ah, but the bard doth speak wisely.

In his delightful play *Twelfth Night,* the love of which Shakespeare writes is romance, the special love of the heart between a man and a woman. In this perceptive line, Shakespeare underscores the joy of a romantic love that flows naturally, without manipulation or coercion, from one to another.

Unfortunately, that romantic joy has departed from far too many marriages. And gentlemen, can we be honest here? Many of us are to blame.

Why is it that, after a passionate courtship and honeymoon, we often let the princely courtesies, romantic gifts, and magic moments become buried by routine?

Possibly it's because familiarity breeds complacency. When the thrill of the chase is over, when we discover that the other hangs the toilet paper backwards, when screaming, wet little "bundles of joy" enter the picture, the passionate fires start to die. Complacency, if unchecked, then becomes boredom.

True, over time the puppy-eyed Romeo in us is bound to give way to a more rational, less emotional, foundation of love. And it should.

But most women, thank the good Lord, are romantic creatures. God has created them with a deep craving to be loved and constantly assured of that love. He made men that way too, but many of us don't like to admit it.

That's why the wedding should not signal the end of the courtship, but the beginning.

Much as women like to hear the words "I love you," they need to see visible expressions of that love. The small, thoughtful gift that says, "I was thinking about you today." Or the little action that tells her she's your favorite person in the whole world.

One of the most delightful discoveries I've made in my marriage to Kathy is that "love given unsought is better." When I take the initiative to verbalize and demonstrate my love for her, our spirits are drawn together and we rediscover the inner laughter of people in love. It's a joy that no man or his wife should ever let slip away from their union.

Over time, I've compiled these discoveries into a list of "101 Ways to Say 'I Love You' to Your Wife." Use them to help start your own creativity flowing.

101 WAYS TO SAY "I LOVE YOU"

1. *Leave love notes for her—at least one per month. Leave them around the house, in her car, in her purse or briefcase.*

2. *Fix a picnic lunch and take her to her favorite spot.*

3. *Phone her during the day just to tell her how much you love and appreciate her. No business talk allowed.*

4. *Tell her, "You're my best friend"—and mean it.*

5. *Give her a backrub without being asked.*

6. *Keep on making "dates" with her throughout your marriage. Ask for a date on Friday night, and arrange for baby-sitters. When you're dressed, slip out of the house and come to the door for her, flowers in hand.*

7. *Laugh at her jokes.*

8. *Plan a "World's Greatest Mom" dinner with the kids. Have them make a trophy, banner, decorations, the works—including testimonials on why their mother is the world's greatest mom. Pitch in with your own testimonial, too.*

9. *Make her a valentine anytime during the year.*

10. *Follow this guideline in your house: "I won't sit down till she can sit down." In other words, make kitchen work and housework a shared responsibility, a partnership. Use this work time together for conversation, jokes, and affirmations.*

11. *Write her a poem expressing your feelings about something intimate between the two of you. A warm memory. A recent walk together. An argument that, when settled, helped draw you closer together. The beauty, love, or skill you observe in her.*

12. *Surprise her with breakfast in bed. And not just on her birthday or Mother's Day. If she asks "What's the occasion?" as you fluff her pillows behind her, just smile and say, "No particular reason . . . I just love you."*

13. *Warm her side of the bed before she gets in.*

14. *Bring home her favorite frozen yogurt.*

15. *Say, "Honey, I need your advice."*

16. *A few years ago, for Valentine's Day, I bought a box of large, empty gelatin capsules at the drugstore. Then I counted out fifty-two capsules and on a sheet of paper wrote fifty-two one-liners such as:*

"One movie of your choice with yours truly"
"Three consecutive nights' total freedom from kitchen duties"
"One pizza with the works on the evening of your choice"
"One long walk together"
"One leisurely breakfast out together"
"One new blouse of your choice"
"One sexy new outfit (of my choice)."

Some involved spending money; others merely time, but each meant a special treat for her. I took a pair of scissors to the sheet, then rolled up each note and inserted one into each capsule.

When Kathy opened the little package, the prescription on the bottle read, *Rx from Dr. Dan Benson for Kathy Benson. To prevent dull marriage, take one capsule every week for the next year.*

The gift meant many fun times together. Half the fun was watching Kathy continually fight off the urge to open them all at once.

17. *Read a book together.*

18. *Accept her folks, warts and all. Take initiative to show and tell them you love them.*

19. *Give her frequent "space" breaks—opportunities to get away from you, the house, the children, her job, and blow off steam. Fill the tank of her car with gas and tell her you'll watch the kids. Her only responsibility for the day is to go out and have fun.*

20. *Phone her at home or at her job and arrange to meet during the day for lunch. Use this time to talk about your life together, plans for the family and the future, or anything that's on her mind.*

21. *Serve her during mealtime. Many wives, and most mothers, are forced to eat their food cold because they are constantly hopping up from the table to serve everyone's needs. Let her sit and enjoy the food for once while you get another napkin for Junior or more iced tea for yourself. Teach your kids to also practice this servant spirit.*

22. *Kiss her passionately in front of the kids.*

23. *Make a card with a "love acrostic" of her name. Conclude with this line: Just a few reasons why I love you.*

24. *Some Saturday morning—or a weekday if you can arrange it—write on a slip of paper, "Let's go to the amusement park today" or "Let's go to the beach—just the two of us." Gift wrap it and present it to her with a kiss at breakfast.*

25. *When the two of you are at a party or gathering, catch her eye with a wink and a smile. Let her know that of all the women in the room, she's the most attractive and important to you.*

26. *At the same gathering, take her hand and whisper in her ear, "I can't wait to get you home . . . " She may feign embarrassment, but she'll love it.*

27. *Never, never compare her to old girlfriends, your mom, your sister, or anyone else.*

28. *Keep her car serviced and gassed up for her.*

29. *Make the bed in the morning while she's in the bathroom or fixing breakfast.*

30. *Send her a singing telegram.*

31. *Pray together. Nothing will give her greater security than knowing you are totally dedicated to God and his guidance. Go to him together in thanks, in praise, and in problem solving.*

32. *As you pray together, take her hand and thank God for giving her to you. If you sneak a peek (I doubt that the Lord would mind), you'll probably catch her smiling.*

33. *Make it a policy to never speak negatively of her to another person—in her presence or in her absence. Anything undesirable in the woman you love is strictly between you and her—and should be worked out in loving, honest communication with each other.*

34. *From the next room, call out, "Honey?" When she responds, just say, "I love you." This tells her you're thinking good thoughts about her.*

35. *Remember the partnership. Be alert for all the things you can do to keep the home running smoothly and make things easier on her. If you finish the orange juice, mix a new batch. Replace the empty toilet paper roll. Sweep down a cobweb. Take on the vacuuming.*

36. *Feed the dog.*

37. *Feed the baby.*

38. *Change the diapers (on the baby).*

39. *If Junior has discovered the trick of bawling for Mommy late at night, let Mom rest. She's earned it. Tend to him yourself.*

A BREATH OF FRESH AIR

40. *"Let's go out to dinner."*

41. *"Let's go buy you a new (item of clothing)."*

42. *"Let's go away for the weekend—just the two of us."*

43. *If she's on a diet or fitness binge, encourage her. Fat jokes are definitely out. If you see improvement, however slight, be sure to tell her. "Honey, you're looking better and better" will bring a smile and renewed determination on her part. And while she's at it, why not join her?*

44. *Purchase a car emergency kit for her car, and give her an auto club membership and a supply of quarters for emergency calls.*

45. *Say, "I really enjoy being with you."*

46. *Tell your children often, privately, how much you love their mother. Then let them see it in action every day. If you treat her like a queen, they'll want to, too.*

47. *Scheme with the kids on creative ways to surprise Mom—plan and prepare a meal, clean the house when she's gone, make a special gift, or plan a "Queen for a Day" celebration.*

48. *Turn the phones off before and during family meals and during your intimate times in the bedroom.*

49. *Never let hand-holding become a thing of the past. It's one of those little things she'll never grow tired of. In sitting or walking together,*

take her hand proudly. (Exception: Avoid the above when she's drying her nail polish. Your affections won't be duly appreciated.)

50. *Be adventurous! Try new restaurants. Explore new pathways or resort towns. Pick a new recreational activity and go for it.*

51. *Compliment her.*

52. *Show interest in her activities and work. Ask questions to show you really want to know her world better.*

UNSPECIAL OCCASIONS

53. *Birthdays and anniversaries, of course, are special occasions and should always be commemorated as such (write them on your personal calendar at the start of every year.) But try these little surprises for no special occasion:*

A single long-stemmed rose
A bouquet or plant delivered to her at her place of work or at home
A slinky nightgown (shopping for it is half the fun)
A tape or CD of her favorite musical performer
A video she's been wanting to see
A scented candle or potpourri
A helium-filled balloon
A perfume she likes
A romantic or humorous greeting card
A craft which you, she, and the kids can work on together
A ring, necklace, earrings, or bracelet
A book she's been wanting to read
A new photo of you.

M
A
N
T
A
L
K

HOMEMADE SURPRISES

54. *Even better, surprise her with something
      you've made yourself.*
      A plaque
      A sculpture or pottery
      A painting
      *A greeting card with original poetry and art-
        work*
      A scented candle
      A framed photograph of a scene or cute animal.

BE IMPRACTICAL

55. *When it comes to Christmas, birthdays, or
     anniversaries, forget the practical stuff. Don't
     even think about a new toaster or iron. Those
     are household items, not love gifts. (Would
     you have bought her such things when you
     were dating her?) Use these times of the year
     to find the creative little extravagances that
     tell her she's well worth a splurge.*
56. *Phone her when you're delayed in coming
     home from work or other engagements.*
57. *Leave the toilet seat down when you're
     through in the bathroom.*
58. *Arrange with her well in advance of invit-
     ing a friend home to dinner. Ask her; don't
     tell her.*
59. *Say, "You're sure a good lover."*

MAD MONEY AND OTHER DELIGHTS

60. *In your mutual financial planning allot her
     a personal spending allowance equal to (or
     greater than) yours, to do with as she chooses.*
61. *Make sure you have an up-to-date will and
     adequate life, health, and disability insurance*

to provide for her and the kids if something should happen to you.

62. Organize a notebook for her that explains where all the essential family records (mortgage, insurance policies, tax and investment records) are kept and who to contact if something should happen to you.

63. Give her a foot rub.

64. Let her sleep in.

65. Renew your wedding vows.

66. When you both arrive home at the end of the day, search her out and give her a big, prolonged hug first thing. Show her that seeing her is the best part of your day.

67. Set aside a few minutes, a half-hour, or more each day just to visit with her. Make it a time when the kids are busy or in bed, when chores are over and you're both starting to unwind from the day. Turn the phones off and talk together about the things on each other's minds . . . about goals . . . about dreams. Make a special effort to listen to, encourage, and affirm this special woman God has given you.

68. Don't allow even your favorite houseguests to pull you away from this time together. An extended stay by Jack and Julie is when your wife may need to be alone with you the most.

69. Compliment her on her intelligence.

70. Sing her praises! Tell others what you appreciate about your wife. Go beyond physical attributes and practical skills—praise her character qualities as well.

71. If you must go out of town, hide little love treasures around the house for her to discover. A romantic card under her pillow. A

chocolate truffle on her desk. A bookmark in her Bible. A love note propped in front of her dressing mirror.

72. True, home is to be lived in. But slobdom has no place in ongoing courtship, and let's face it, the way some of us dress and behave at home can be as romantic to her as hair rollers and flannel nightgowns are to us. Be comfortable, but pay some attention to your appearance and manners just as you did when you were dating her.

73. Hire a plane to tow a love message over a public gathering.

74. In a group discussion, ask, "What do you think, Honey?"

75. Chalk a heart with your names in it on your patio or front sidewalk.

76. Take her picture in her favorite outfit. Take another of her in your favorite outfit.

77. Try to accompany her when she goes grocery shopping, or do the shopping yourself. It's a big, thankless job, and parking lots aren't really safe for women shopping alone.

78. Give her a lesson or class in something she's always wanted to learn.

79. Try to be consistent in expressing sincere appreciation for the contribution she makes around the house. Notice the rooms that are straightened and vacuumed, your ironed shirts, the aroma of what's cooking. Compliment and thank her as you give her a warm hug. Try to never take her hard work for granted. (Coach the kids on this one, too!)

CHIVALRY IS ALIVE AND WELL

Three statements she'll never grow tired of hearing:

80. *"You sure are looking good today."*
81. *"I'm sure glad you're my wife."*
82. *"You're my favorite person in the whole world."*
83. *Over the phone, by mail, or in person, tell her parents how much you love their daughter. Thank them for the great job they did raising her and for letting you marry her.*
84. *Watch for the smile in her eyes when you dust off some of those "manners" which some of us abandoned shortly after the wedding:*

    Open her car door for her (even if she's the driver).
    Help seat her at the dinner table.
    After you've seated her, give her a kiss on the cheek and whisper, "I love you."
    Open doors for her, letting her enter first.
    While walking with her, walk on the most hazardous side.

85. *Surprise her with some extra "mad money."*
86. *Empty the trash without her having to ask.*
87. *Let her know that her phone calls are always welcome while you're at the office. Tell your receptionist or secretary that calls from your wife or kids should always be put through to you.*
88. *If you haven't already, abandon the old male habit of joking about the intelligence of women, women drivers, women talkers, women shoppers. She's a woman, and these baseless slurs are also a slur on her.*

M A N T A L K

89. Help her keep the family correspondence going.
90. Compliment her on her mothering.
91. Admire a sunset with her. Or a sunrise.

NINE SIGNS OF A WINNER

92. Memorize Galatians 5:22-23, the apostle Paul's listing of the "fruit of the Spirit." Each day, ask God to help you exercise these nine qualities in your relationship with your wife.
93. Love: always seeking the best for her. Realizing that the opposite of love is not hate, but self. Putting her feelings and interests before your own.
94. Joy: an inner happiness so deeply rooted that it is not swayed by the whims of circumstance. An optimistic outlook on the future and a positive spirit even when things go wrong. Rejoicing in victory. Optimistic in adversity.
95. Peace: a quiet assurance, in spite of circumstances, that God who loves both of you is also seeking the best for you.
96. Patience: always giving her the benefit of the doubt. Putting yourself in her place.
97. Kindness: giving of yourself simply to bring joy to her. Watching for ways to make her load lighter.
98. Goodness: creating an atmosphere in which evil is conspicuously out of place. The foundational attitude from which acts of kindness flow.
99. Faithfulness: fidelity in body, mind and spirit, motivated by an irrevocable, unconditional love for her.

100. *Gentleness: humility born of strength and confidence. Tenderness born of love and best-friendship.*

101. *Self-control: not allowing any activity or appetite to displace God or her in your affections. Staying calm in the midst of the storms. Temperate in diet, spending, work, and play.*

TELL HER "I LOVE YOU" EVERY DAY

To keep your married love fun and fulfilling, never, never let the courtship end. Keep romancing your special lady as if you were trying to win her for the very first time. Don't get discouraged if she doesn't notice a difference at first—she may need some time to get over the shock.

Tell her "I love you" every day. Then back up your words with the ideas I've suggested. Gradually, you'll notice that your love and admiration for her are growing even stronger. There'll be a new liveliness to your interaction, a new sense of adventure to your relationship. You'll almost feel like you're honeymooning again, only now your love and respect for each other will be far deeper.

TAKING ACTION

☐ *Select one idea that says "I love you" and do it for her before the day is over.*

☐ *Choose two more ideas to surprise her during the next week. On what days will you do each one?*

☐ *Memorize Galatians 5:22-23, the apostle Paul's list of the "fruit of the Spirit." Ask God to help you remember and exercise these nine qualities in your relationships—especially with your wife.*

M
A
N
T
A
L
K

NOTES

CHAPTER 2

1. Author-speaker Cavett Robert attended the businessmen's luncheon at which Will Rogers spoke these words. Robert wrote about the experience in *Human Engineering and Motivation* (Englewood Cliffs, NJ: Parker Publishing Co., 1969).

CHAPTER 4

1. This statement was made by Clarence Randall, then president of Inland Steel, and quoted by Dan Benson in *The Total Man* (Wheaton, IL: Tyndale House Publishers, 1977), p. 24.

CHAPTER 6

1. These statistics are from a Reader's Digest/Gallup Survey conducted in 1983.
2. C. Northcote Parkinson, *The Law and the Profits* (Boston: Houghton Mifflin, 1960).

CHAPTER 8

1. William Ecenbarger, "Plastic Is as Good as Gold," *Philadelphia Inquirer*, January 24, 1988.
2. Daniel M. Kehrer, "How to Cut Out Debt," *Changing Times*, April 1988.
3. "When You're Too Far in Debt," *Money*, April 1987.
4. Ibid.
5. Kehrer, "How to Cut Out Debt," *Changing Times*, April 1988.

CHAPTER 9

1. Edward Yardeni, chief economist at Prudential-Bache Securities, quoted by Marguerite T. Smith, "Great Moves to Make Your Savings Grow," *Money*, February 1990.
2. This statement summarizes Social Security Administration statistics quoted by financial consultant Ron Blue in *Master Your Money* (Nashville, TN: Thomas Nelson Publishers, 1988).
3. Leonard Wiener, "Cultivating a Savings Habit," *U.S. News & World Report*, 14 August 1989.

4. George S. Clason, *The Richest Man in Babylon* (Spring Valley, NY: Hawthorn Press, Elsevier-Dutton Publishing Co., first published in 1926).

CHAPTER 10
1. Dennis and Barbara Rainey, *Building Your Mate's Self-Esteem* (San Bernardino, CA: Here's Life Publishers, 1986), p. 27.

CHAPTER 13
1. Howard Markman's research is reported by Karen S. Peterson in "Husbands Want to Fight by the Rules," *USA Today,* 27 October 1989, p. 1-D.

CHAPTER 14
1. Shere Hite's research is quoted by Myron Harris and Jane Norman in *The Private Life of the American Teenager* (New York: Rawson, Wade Publishers, 1981).

M

A

N

T

A

L

K